Advanced WordPress Security

By Grant Stokley

Published by Grant Stokley
gingsoft.com

ISBN: 9798674242178

Table of Contents

Conventions used in this book

The following typographical conventions are being used in this book

- **Bold**
    - Exact names for things that you should be seeing in the browser.
- `Mono-spaced`
    - Is for code or command line
- …
    - Three dots are used to identify where the output of logs, source code, or configuration files have been truncated to make it easier to locate the subject matter.

Introduction

This book goes beyond the basics and dives into more advanced defenses. I'll show you how to surgically replace WordPress PHP code with a deceptive modification. The attacker can brute force every possible password, and never know which one is correct. You don't need to be a developer; I'll show you step by step. I'll show you how to hide your username from common enumeration techniques, so the attacker won't even know which user's password to attack.

I'll show you how to stop ongoing attacks then blacklist the attacker. For a more secure approach, use whitelists, user-agent strings combinations, and a 2FA plugin. Plugins are like trojan horses, they provide functionality for you and the attacker. I'll show you how to use free tools that perform static and dynamic application security testing (aka SAST & DAST) on the plugins, so you can avoid installing risky plugins that compromise your WordPress site.

Have you ever wagered on the Kentucky Derby? If you have, then you might be familiar with the online advanced deposit wagering platform, twinspires.com. That website and mobile application will accept your money, allow you to place your bets, and pays you when you are a winner. On Derby Day, tens of thousands of registrations, deposits, and wagering transactions happen every minute leading up to the big race. There is a lot riding on that application.

I was a member of the Information Security Team (aka InfoSec) at Churchill Downs Inc. focused on application security for twinspires.com. Before moving into that role, I was a software developer for twinspires.com. So, I have a deep understanding of what it takes to secure web applications on multiple levels from the code itself, the servers it runs on, the networks that are traversed, all the way out to the Web Application Firewall. I'm giving you my application security experience in this book.

Chapter 1 | Configuring Access Control

Overview

Apache access control can be configured using either the directory level .htaccess files or apache2.conf, the main Apache configuration. You can allow or deny based on partial or full IP addresses, subnets, domain names, and even environment variables such as user-agent string.

Allow, Deny, & Order

To give you some context as to what this looks like, Figure 1-1 is an example of a Directory directive in the apache2.conf file.

FIGURE 1-1 *Use of Directives*

```
<Directory /var/www/html/devsite/>
        AllowOverride None
        Order Allow,Deny
        Allow from 111.2.3.45
        Deny from all
</Directory>
```

There are three directives that you will use to configure access control. The **Allow** directive identifies which hosts can access the directory. Conversely, the **Deny** directive identifies which hosts will be denied access to the directory. The **Order** directive sets the default state to be either a whitelist or a blacklist configuration.

FIGURE 1-2 *Default action is to deny*

```
# ============================
# Whitelisting internal subnets
# Denying everyone else
# ============================
<Directory /var/www/html>
        AllowOverride None
        Order Allow,Deny
        Allow from 10.0.0.0/24
        Allow from 10.0.1.0/24
</Directory>
```


An example use case for the **Order** directive might be something like Figure 1-2. During the development, you take a whitelist approach by allowing only the subnets where the system administrator and developer hosts reside and deny all other hosts. When the site is finally ready to be released, you will reverse the order of the directives and allow all hosts, except for known bad actors, like in Figure 1-3.

FIGURE 1-3 *Default action is to allow*

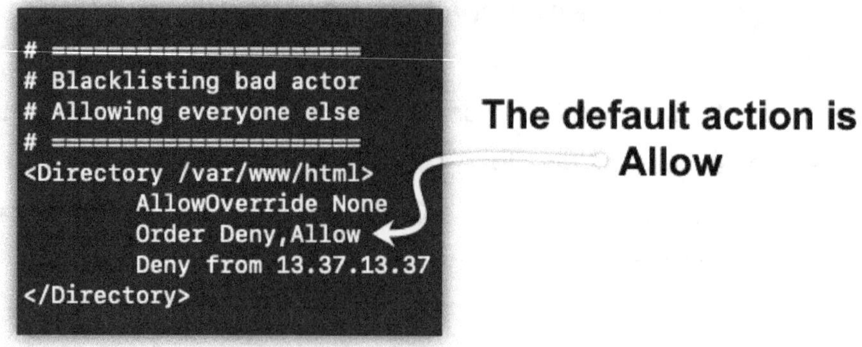

```
# ============================
# Blacklisting bad actor
# Allowing everyone else
# ============================
<Directory /var/www/html>
        AllowOverride None
        Order Deny,Allow
        Deny from 13.37.13.37
</Directory>
```

Access Control Rules

The rules are relatively straight forward when evaluating for access control:

- All rules will be evaluated, regardless of an early match. This is counterintuitive if you've ever configured access control lists in firewalls.
- If the requesting host doesn't match in either **Allow** or **Deny**, the default action is taken.
- The last directive is the default action.
    - If you chose **Allow,Deny** the default action is to *deny* if no match is found in either the **Allow** or **Deny** directives.
    - If you chose **Deny,Allow** the default action is to *allow* if no match is found in either the **Deny** or **Allow** directives.
- There cannot be any whitespace between the Allow and Deny directives being set (only a comma). The syntax is **Order Allow,Deny** or **Order Deny,Allow**.
- Changes require a restart, **apache2ctl restart**

Syntax for the Allow and Deny directives

To create an access control rule, follow these syntax rules:

- Use **from** before you designate the target of the rule (e.g. **Allow from** or **Deny from**).
- The target can be full domain names (e.g. Allow from **awpsec.com**).
- The target can be partial domain names (e.g. Deny from **.com**).
- The target can be IPv4 or IPv6 addresses (e.g. Deny from **13.37.13.37**).
- The target can be partial IPv4 or IPv6 addresses (e.g. Allow from **10.0.0**).
- The target can be network/subnet mask (e.g. Deny from **13.37.13.0/255.255.255.0**).

- The target can be a CIDR notation (e.g. Allow from **10.0.0.0/24**).
- The target can be all (e.g. Allow from **all**).
- The target can be an environment variable (e.g. Allow from **env=siprnet_user**).

In Figure 1-4, you can check your configuration files for syntax errors without starting the server by using **sudo apache2ctl configtest** or just **sudo apache2ctl -t** command line option.

Figure 1-4 *apache2ctl*

```
root@ip-172-31-14-82:~# apache2ctl -t
Syntax OK
root@ip-172-31-14-82:~# apache2ctl configtest
Syntax OK
```

Troubleshooting Example

You are in the development stage of building the website. No one (Deny from all) but you (Allow from 111.2.3.45) should have access to it. You have read this far and have implemented the Directory directive that you think will work similar to Figure 1-5.

FIGURE 1-5 *Double deny issue*

```
<Directory /var/www/html/devsite/>
        AllowOverride None
        Order Allow,Deny
        Allow from 111.2.3.45
        Deny from all
</Directory>
```

You restart Apache2 so the changes you made take effect, by typing **apache2ctl restart**.

```
apache2ctl restart
```

You hop over to the browser and receive an error like this is Figure 1-6.

FIGURE 1-6 *Forbidden error from Apache*

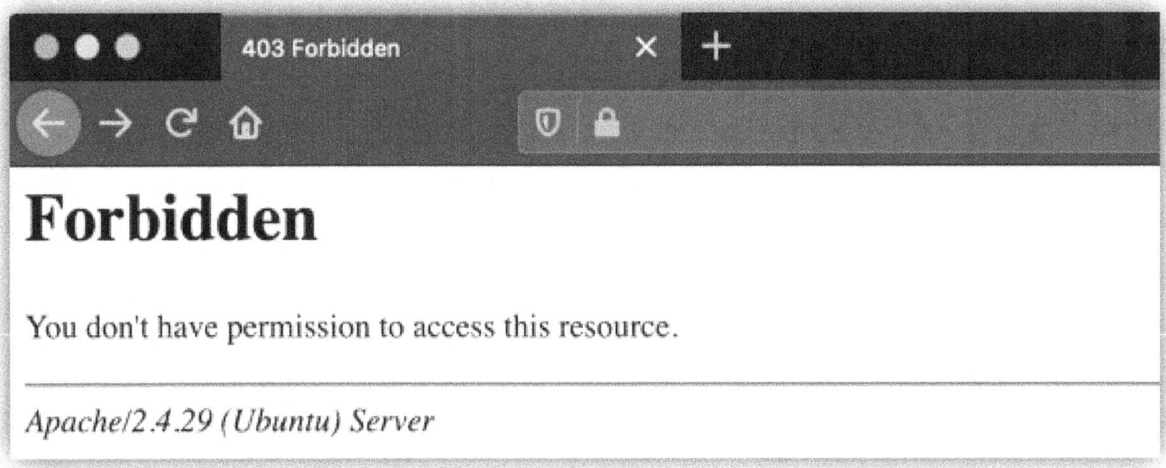

You go back, triple check everything, character by character. You run the syntax check, **sudo apache2ctl configtest**.

```
sudo apache2ctl configtest
```

It returns with **Syntax OK**. Next step, you remember the logs. Maybe something in there will give you a clue.

```
sudo tail /var/log/apache2/error.log
```

You find an entry similar to Figure 1-7 in the error.log file.

FIGURE 1-7 *Allowed IP is denied*

```
[Mon May 04 12:41:14.482986 2020] [access_compat:error] [pid 7989]
[client 111.2.3.45:54964] AH01797: client denied by server configur
ation: /var/www/html/devsite
```

It looks like you are getting denied by server configuration. You know it's hitting the intended directive, because it listed it by the path (/var/www/html/devsite). The IP address matches the Allow directive, so why is it being denied? Look at Figure 1-8.

FIGURE 1-8 *Flow diagram for evaluating directives*

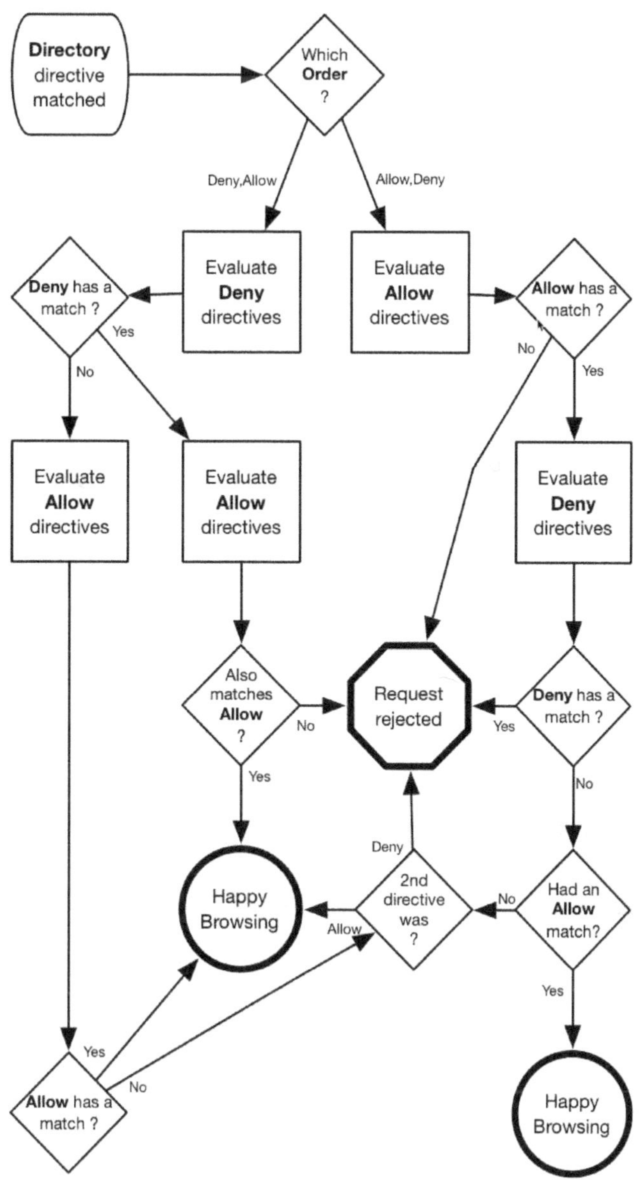

The **Directory** directive did match given the results you saw in the error.log file. Moving onto the diamond named, "Which Order ?". You have chosen **Allow,Deny**, so follow the branch down to the right.

```
<Directory /var/www/html/devsite/>
     AllowOverride None
     Order Allow,Deny
     Allow from 111.2.3.45
     Deny from all
</Directory>
```

At the "Evaluate Allow directives" box, look at the **Allow from 111.2.3.45** rule.

```
<Directory /var/www/html/devsite/>
     AllowOverride None
     Order Allow,Deny
     Allow from 111.2.3.45
     Deny from all
</Directory>
```

That is considered a match because that is your IP address and it matches in the **error.log** file. At the "Allow has a match ?" diamond, you take the *Yes* path since it was a match.

The *Yes* path brings you to the "Evaluate Deny directives" box. Here you have a **Deny from all** rule.

```
<Directory /var/www/html/devsite/>
    AllowOverride None
    Order Allow,Deny
    Allow from 111.2.3.45
    Deny from all
</Directory>
```

If you are following along on the flow diagram. This is where the light bulb comes on over your head. The **Deny from all** will always match. So, if you follow the *Yes* path again, you notice that your requests will always be rejected. In other words, the **Allow from 111.222.33.44** entry will never matter as long as the **Deny from all** rule is there and Deny is the default. In Figure 1-9, if you remove the **Deny from all** rule, only requests from 111.2.3.45 will be accepted because it matches an Allow rule and no longer matches a Deny rule.

FIGURE 1-9 *Remove the Deny from all entry*

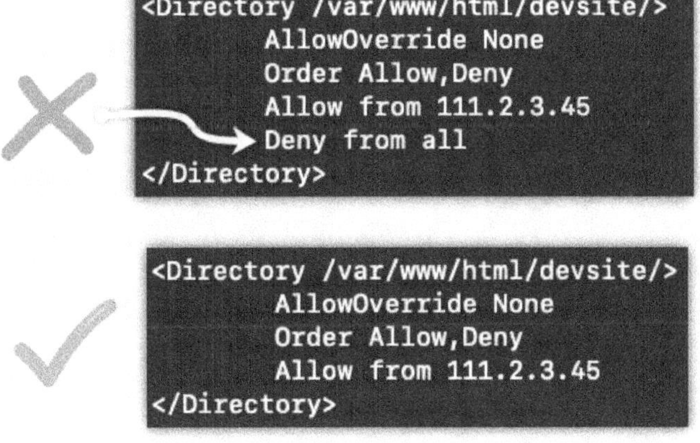

The other hosts will not match a Allow rule, nor a Deny rule, and will fall into the default action. In this case, the default action is a Deny. Save the **apache2.conf** file and restart Apache. Verify this works by checking from the IP in the **Allow from 111.2.3.45** rule and a different IP address.

Summary

You should now have a basic understanding of the rules and syntax using the Allow, Deny and Order directives. You will use that knowledge to block unwanted traffic. Refer back to the flow diagram and your log files when you are troubleshooting allowed and denied traffic.

Chapter 2 | Apache Configuration

Overview

In order to defend against attacks aimed at your WordPress site, you need to defend the Apache web server that it is running on. You will locate the main Apache configuration file and identify key components such as the environment variables and where the log files are stored.

Where is Apache Configured?

The first thing that you have to do is locate where on this Linux server is the Apache service running from. Services on Ubuntu are in the **/lib/systemd/system** directory. Obviously, if you are running a different flavor of Linux it could be in a different directory. There are hundreds of services in the /lib/systemd/system directory, but you are only interested in apache2. Type **ls -la apache2*** in the console.

```
cd /lib/systemd/system
ls -la apache2*
```

The result is…

```
-rw-r--r-- 1 root root  346 Jul 16  2019 apache2.service
-rw-r--r-- 1 root root  418 Jul 16  2019 apache2@.service

apache2.service.d:
total 44
drwxr-xr-x  2 root root  4096 Apr 17 02:48 .
```

```
drwxr-xr-x 23 root root 36864 May 14 06:51 ..
-rw-r--r--  1 root root    42 Jul 16  2019 apache2-systemd.conf
```

Let's peek into the first file, apache2.service. Type **cat apache2.service** in the console.

```
cat apache2.service
```

The contents of the apache2.service file…

```
[Unit]
Description=The Apache HTTP Server
After=network.target remote-fs.target nss-lookup.target

[Service]
Type=forking
Environment=APACHE_STARTED_BY_SYSTEMD=true
ExecStart=/usr/sbin/apachectl start
ExecStop=/usr/sbin/apachectl stop
ExecReload=/usr/sbin/apachectl graceful
PrivateTmp=true
Restart=on-abort

[Install]
WantedBy=multi-user.target
cat /usr/sbin/apachectl
```

Notice in the **apache2.service** file that there is a reference to the **/usr/sbin/apachectl** file, which also has parameters passed into it like start, stop, and graceful. Type **cat /usr/sbin/apache2ctl** in the console to view the file.

```
cat /usr/sbin/apache2ctl
```

This is a big script, so you will have to scroll back up to fine the beginning of it. If you look around the 45th line or so, you will see where this script identifies the main configuration directory in a variable named APACHE_CONFDIR.

```
. . .
# main configuration directory
if test -z "$APACHE_CONFDIR" ; then
      if test "${0##*apache2ctl-}" != "$0" ; then
            APACHE_CONFDIR="/etc/apache2-${0##*apache2ctl-}"
      else
            APACHE_CONFDIR=/etc/apache2
      fi
fi
. . .
```

The value of that variable is **/etc/apache2**. This is where you will configure Apache.

Main Apache Configuration File

The file in the **/etc/apache2** directory that is of great interest to us, is the **apache2.conf** file. Depending on the version of Apache that you are running, the file might be named **httpd.conf** instead. There are lots of commented lines in this file. To see what actionable commands are in the file, grep out the lines with a **#** symbol. From the results, here are the items to focus on. To save paper, '…' will be used in place of lots of irrelevant text.

```
cat apache2.conf | grep -v '#'
```

```
...
User ${APACHE_RUN_USER}
Group ${APACHE_RUN_GROUP}
...
```

Here is where the variables for **User** and **Group** from the **envvars** file get used. Also notice the **Include** statements for other configuration files.

```
...
Include ports.conf
...
IncludeOptional conf-enabled/*.conf
...
IncludeOptional sites-enabled/*.conf
...
```

Notice there are XML type nodes in the file referring to directory locations. They are called directives in Apache. If you look at the last **Directory** directive, it's referring to **/var/www**.

```
<Directory />
```

```
    Options FollowSymLinks
    AllowOverride None
    Require all denied
</Directory>

<Directory /usr/share>
    AllowOverride None
    Require all granted
</Directory>

<Directory /var/www/>
    Options Indexes FollowSymLinks
    AllowOverride None
    Require all granted
</Directory>
```

Further down we run across this statement naming **.htaccess** as the **AccessFileName**. This is an important line from a security perspective. In fact, it's the topic of the next chapter.

```
...
AccessFileName .htaccess
...
```

Environment Variables

In the **/etc/apache2** directory there is a file named **envvars**, which contains the environment variables for Apache. To locate variables, look for the export command followed by the

<variable_name>=<value>. Here are a couple variables, **APACHE_RUN_USER** and **APACHE_RUN_GROUP**.

```
export APACHE_RUN_USER=www-data
export APACHE_RUN_GROUP=www-data
```

Notice the **www-data** user and group names that Apache is using.

Another variable that we need to know about is the **APACHE_LOG_DIR**. The Apache logs play a big part in security. Without these logs, we are blind to who is attacking the server. Here you can see that the variable is set to **/var/log/apache2**.

```
export APACHE_LOG_DIR=/var/log/apache2$SUFFIX
```

A common attack against WordPress, is to exploit the **xmlrpc.php** file. If we peek at the tail end of the log file and grep it for **xmlrpc.php**, we can already see attempts to exploit it.

```
tail /var/log/apache2/access.log | grep xmlrpc.php

34.248.44.207 - - [30/June/2020:12:21:35 +0000] "POST /xmlrpc.php HTTP/1.1"
200 3491
103.48.193.152 - - [30/June/2020:12:34:19 +0000] "POST /xmlrpc.php HTTP/1.1"
200 439
```

With the log file, you can see that 34.248.44.207 and 103.48.193.152 both made POST requests. The 200 toward the end of the log entry, is the HTTP status code for OK. We will dive deeper into the logs later. The intent here was to show you how to find the logs.

Summary

We identified apache2.conf as the main Apache configuration file. This revealed the www-data as the Apache user and www-data as the Apache group name. The directory directives, other locations for configuration files, along with the location of the log files.

Chapter 3 | The .htaccess File

Overview

The most common way to configure access control in Apache are via the .htaccess files. However, you may be able to simplify the configuration and use the main Apache configuration file instead.

Multiple .htaccess Files

The .htaccess file provides a method of making *per-directory* configuration changes. Typically, this is how access control for Apache is configured. Remember from the last chapter, that the main Apache configuration file, apache2.conf, made reference to the .htaccess file. You could actually change this filename if you wanted. However, some WordPress plugins will look for the .htaccess file by name during their install process and may fail to install if it's missing.

As far as the per-directory aspect, there can be multiple .htaccess files. You could have one in each subdirectory. If you are running multiple websites from the same server, each will have their own .htaccess file, or multiple .htaccess files depending on the directory structure.

Avoid Using .htaccess Files

Here is a performance tip for you. Do not use .htaccess files if you can help it. Instead, use the Directory directive in the apache2.conf file. When AllowOverride directive is set (Figure 3-1) to a value other than none, Apache will need to look in every subdirectory for .htaccess files, whether or not you actually even use them.

FIGURE 3-1 *AllowOverride*

To make it worse, the .htaccess file is loaded into memory every time a document is requested. Complexity is always bad for security. Using multiple hierarchical files to implement security will be complicated and sometimes confusing since you have to go upstream into the main Apache configuration file to allow downstream files to be overridden in the first place. Then one .htaccess can be downstream of another, the same process has to happen again, and each subdirectory after, may or may not need to be modified depending on why the directory exists. At some point human nature sets in and you accidently allow access to something that you didn't mean to. All of this complexity goes away, if you just do all of the configuration in one place, the main Apache configuration file.

Summary

Try to configure the access control in the Directory directives in the apache2.conf file. That keeps it simple and easy to deal with since it's all controlled in a single location. I said, "try to," because some plugins that you may choose to install later may require the .htaccess file to exist in order to function. So, you may not be able to avoid using the .htaccess files, so be careful when dealing with them.

Chapter 4 | Block Username Enumeration

Overview

There are multiple methods used by attackers to discover what your administrator account is. Unfortunately, you have to block all of them. Not all attackers are created equal. Motivation, tradecraft, intent, and skill level all play a part.

Novice attackers are not even aware of all of the methods built into WordPress, that are available to them to retrieve the username. They will google for hacking WordPress or something similar. Then attempt what they found on the first page of results on the first unsuspecting target that comes to mind. When it fails, they move on to another target using that same method.

Most of the attacks against your WordPress website will be automated scripts ran by bots that attempt attacks on every WordPress website on the Internet. Within minutes of you releasing your website to the public, it will be hit with a HTTP GET request from seemingly random IP address. Later in this book, we will be looking at those.

Then there is the persistent attacker who is targeting you specifically. There are many forms of this attacker.

- It could be a hacktivist who perceives injustice with something you or your company has done or posted and is compelled and highly motivated to do damage.
- It could be an ex-employee who thinks they were treated unfairly, passed over for promotion, or terminated by a boss they hated.

- It could be your competition. By eliminating you, they acquire more market share. If you have a perceived security breach, they can scare customers away from you.

Persistent attackers will use every possible method to gain access. Therefore, it's important to defend against every method that you can.

Method 1, author parameter

There is an easier way to figure out what the name your administrator user account is, rather than guessing it.   More skilled attackers will just ask WordPress to tell them what it is. If you type **/?author=1** after the domain name in the URL address bar in your browser, like this…

```
https://yourwpwebsite.com/?author=1
```

You will be redirected to a URL containing the user_login name of the 1st WordPress user. The 1st user in every WordPress installation is the administrator user. Let's say for example that you aren't using the default **admin** name, instead you are using **spaceghost**, so as a result **spaceghost** will appears in the URL after the redirect.

```
https://yourwpwebsite.com/author/spaceghost/
```

Effectively, it's like running a MySQL query directly from the URL bar of your browser. In Figure 4-1, the **author** parameter in the query string (after the **?**), is referring to the **user_login** field in the **wp_users** table. When you also pass in the ID that you are looking for, with **=1**. You get the same answer as you would have if you would have queried the MySQL database for it.

FIGURE 4-1 *Query string parameter matches database ID*

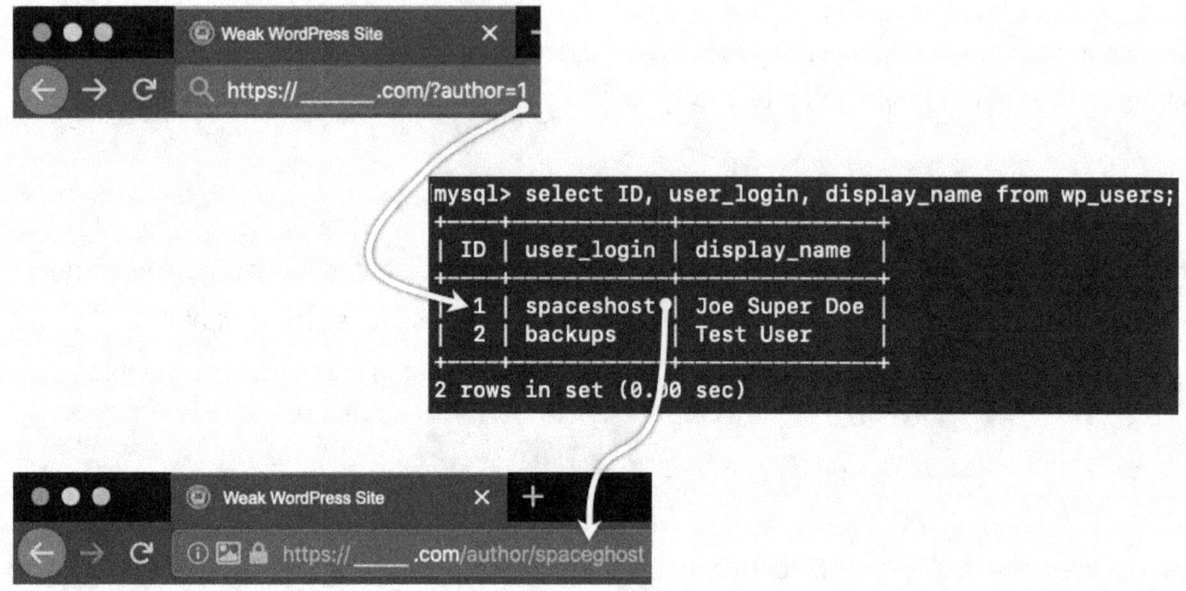

Defense for Method 1, redirect if author is in the query string

The objective is to intercept the **author** parameter in the query string. You will have Apache redirect it to someplace safe, like the **about** page for example. Here is what the configuration looks like.

```
RewriteEngine On
RewriteCond %{QUERY_STRING} author=\d
RewriteRule (.*) about [L,R=301,QSD]
```

You will add those lines into the root directory's **.htaccess file** or your **apache2.conf** file, depending on which method that you've chosen for access control. That seems a pretty straight forward task, but you will probably have to make several attempts, testing, and troubleshooting to get this working. The reason being, there are probably existing rules already in place, and the order of the rules is important. If you place this code in the wrong order, the wrong file, or even the wrong context, it will be passed over without executing.

As another added bonus, you might have to clear your browser's cache in between attempts. I put the code into a place where I knew it should've worked, only to have Chrome lie to me and tell me it wasn't working. Not knowing that, I spent time copying and pasting this code into every possible place. After throwing my hands up, walking away from it for a while, I returned and tried from a different browser and it worked as intended. At that point, I realized I forgot to clear the browser's cache. Don't make the same mistake that I did.

To bypass the browser cache issue all together, just ask for a different author number (ID) each time (e.g. author=2, author=3, author=4, etc.). Don't use the same ID on every attempt while you are testing and troubleshooting (e.g. author=1, author=1, author=1, etc.). The browser cached the response the first time that you requested author=1 and any changes that you are expecting on subsequent requests won't appear.

In Figure 4-2, is what I ended up with as a working configuration in the **.htaccess** file in the /var/www/html directory. Your configuration will most likely be a little different depending on where you are intending to send the attacker.

FIGURE 4-2 *Redirect based on query string*

```
<IfModule mod_rewrite.c>
        RewriteEngine On

        RewriteCond %{QUERY_STRING} author=\d
        RewriteRule (.*) about [L,R=301,QSD]

</IfModule>
```

This will make more sense once you know what each command is doing along with some of the basic rules around where this configuration can live. There is a lot more to the configuration of Apache, I'm only going to scratch the surface to get this defense working.

- **<IfModule mod_rewrite.c>** is effectively saying "If the module, mod_rewrite.c, is loaded then execute commands until you reach **</IfModule>**." The IfModule *can* be used in both apache2.conf and .htaccess files. However, if you are using the apache2.conf file option, you should perform the rewrites in the **Directory** directive instead of IfModule, like in Figure 4-3.

FIGURE 4-3 *Rewrites in the Directory directive*

```
  GNU nano 2.5.3                                File: apache2.conf

<Directory /var/www/html/>
        AllowOverride All
        # Grant Stokley added this but it's not working (check .htaccess)
        # ----------------------------------------------------------------
        RewriteEngine On
        RewriteCond %{QUERY_STRING} author=\d
        RewriteRule (.*) veterans-wall [L,R=301,QSD]
</Directory>
```

- The **RewriteEngine** directive enables (on) or disables (off) the runtime rewriting engine. If set to **off** this module does no runtime processing at all. So, this needs to be set to **on** for URI rewriting to take place.

- The **RewriteCond** statement defines the conditions for the RewriteRule directive that follows.

  - The condition is true if there is a query string in the URI and there is a key named, **author**, and the value is a digit (**\d**).

- The **RewriteRule** statement executes only if the condition is true.

  - The **(.*)** is a regular expression wildcard.

  - **about** is the page where I am sending the attacker. If you look in my apache2.conf attempt, I was sending them to the **veterans-wall** page instead. That was a troubleshooting step, to see which one was working. The point is, you can choose where to send them.

  - The flags [stuff inside the brackets]

    - The **L** flag stands for *last*. If a RewriteRule executes with the L flag set, no further processing of the rule set will happen.

- **R=301** is an R flag set to 301. The R stands for redirect and is meant to issue a redirect to the browser. In our case we are sending the HTTP status code of 301.
- The **QSD** flag causes the query string to be discarded. Which is what you want to do with the attacker's request for your administrator account, discard it!

Method 2, enumeration from the REST API

WordPress provides several Application Programming Interfaces (API). One of which is the REST API. REST, stands for "**RE**presentational **S**tate **T**ransfer." The REST API provides endpoints (as URLs) representing the built-in WordPress data types. An attacker can send and receive JSON data to these endpoints to query, modify and even create content on your site.

JSON is an open standard data format that is human-readable. When you request content from or send content to the API, the response will also be returned in JSON. If you type https://yourwpwebsite.com/**wp-json/wp/v2/users** into your browser, JSON will be returned to you revealing the user_login name again.

```
[{"id":1,"name":"John Super Doe", "url":"","description":"",
"link":"https:\/\/yourwpsebsite.com\/author\/spaceghost\/","slug":"spaceghost
",...
```

Defense for Method 2, redirect requests for users

This is an easy one one-liner! Go back into the apache2.conf or .htaccess that you used previously to defend against Method 1, the query string enumeration against the author. Insert this line before it.

```
RewriteRule ^wp-json/wp/v2/users.*$ - [R=404]
```

Your RewriteRule should look similar to Figure 4-4 now.

FIGURE 4-4 *RewriteRule*

```
  GNU nano 2.5.3                          File: .htaccess

<IfModule mod_rewrite.c>
        RewriteEngine On
        RewriteBase /
        # Added by Grant Stokley to block REST API endpoints
        # ----------------------------------------------------
        RewriteRule ^wp-json/wp/v2/users.*$ - [R=404]

        # Added by Grant Stokley to block author query string
        # ----------------------------------------------------
        RewriteCond %{QUERY_STRING} author=\d
        RewriteRule (.*) about [L,R=301,QSD]




</IfModule>
```

A quick side note, you probably noticed, I add comments to every file that I modify. You should get into this habit so it's easy to find and revert something, should the need arise. This is also handy when revisiting these files after not seeing them for a long period of time, to determine what commands were put there by you, WordPress, or a plugin.

Method 3, brute force using XML-RPC

This is method is more complex and it is the topic of the next chapter…

Summary

By making it harder for the attacker to figure out what your administrative username is. You have added another obstacle that must be overcome before attacks against the password can begin. You defended against the author parameter method of enumeration by redirecting the query to a different page. You also defended the API by returning a HTTP status of 404 when a request for the users is seen by Apache.

Chapter 5 | XML-RPC

Overview

XML-RPC is a Remote Procedure Call (RPC) that passes parameters in an XML format. XML-RPC messages are passed using a HTTP-POST request with the body of the request being XML. No worries, if you are unfamiliar with what a POST request even means, my intent is you to show you the response that xmlrpc.php provides plugin developers as well as the attackers.

What is XML-RPC used for?

The best way to answer that, is to just ask your site what it's used for. You will need a tool that has the capability to make POST requests such as Postman, BurpSuite, browser developer tools, etc. Make a POST request with **system.listMethods** inside the XML node called **methodName** like in Figure 5-1.

FIGURE 5-1 *POST request for system.listMethods*

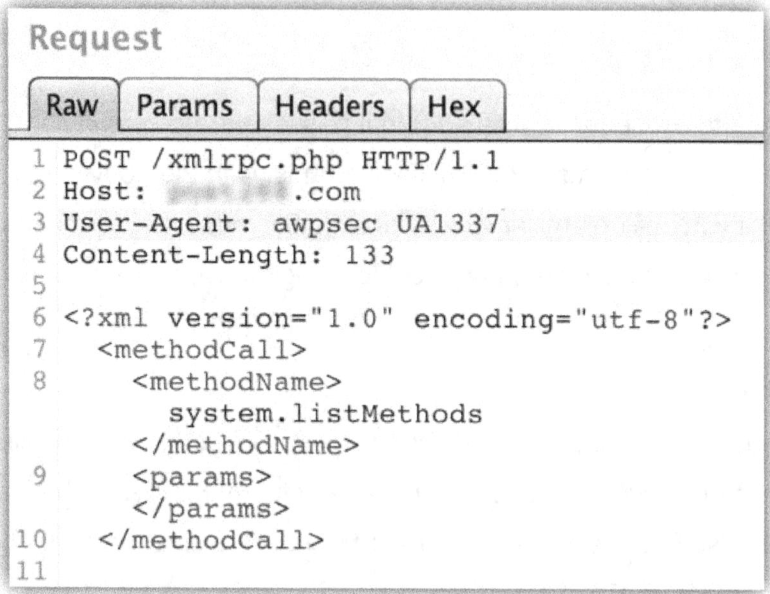


```
 1 POST /xmlrpc.php HTTP/1.1
 2 Host:        .com
 3 User-Agent: awpsec UA1337
 4 Content-Length: 133
 5
 6 <?xml version="1.0" encoding="utf-8"?>
 7   <methodCall>
 8     <methodName>
         system.listMethods
       </methodName>
 9     <params>
       </params>
10   </methodCall>
11
```

After sending the POST request to the server, the response in Figure 5-2 provides a list of the methods that are available via XML-RPC.

FIGURE 5-2 *Response to system.listMethods*

As you can see, there is a lot you can do with XML-RPC. Unfortunately, you can see where this is headed, this can also be used for malicious purposes by an attacker.

How Attackers use XML-RPC to Brute Force logins

By using the **system.multicall** method of XML-RPC, the attacker is able to pack hundreds usernames and password combinations into a single request (aka the payload). To make matters worse the attackers request receives a status of 200 OK, because it is a valid request, even though the payload requests are failing authentication and receiving HTTP status 403 (Forbidden) errors.

Figure 5-3 is an example of exploiting **system.multicall** with a with a brute force payload aimed at the **admin** user account. The attacker is calling the **wp.getAuthors** method each time, just to make it a valid multicall format, but any of the other methods produce the same effect. Notice that the password guess is different each time (e.g. january2020, february2020, December-2021, etc.).

FIGURE 5-3 *Exploiting system.multicall to brute force admin password*

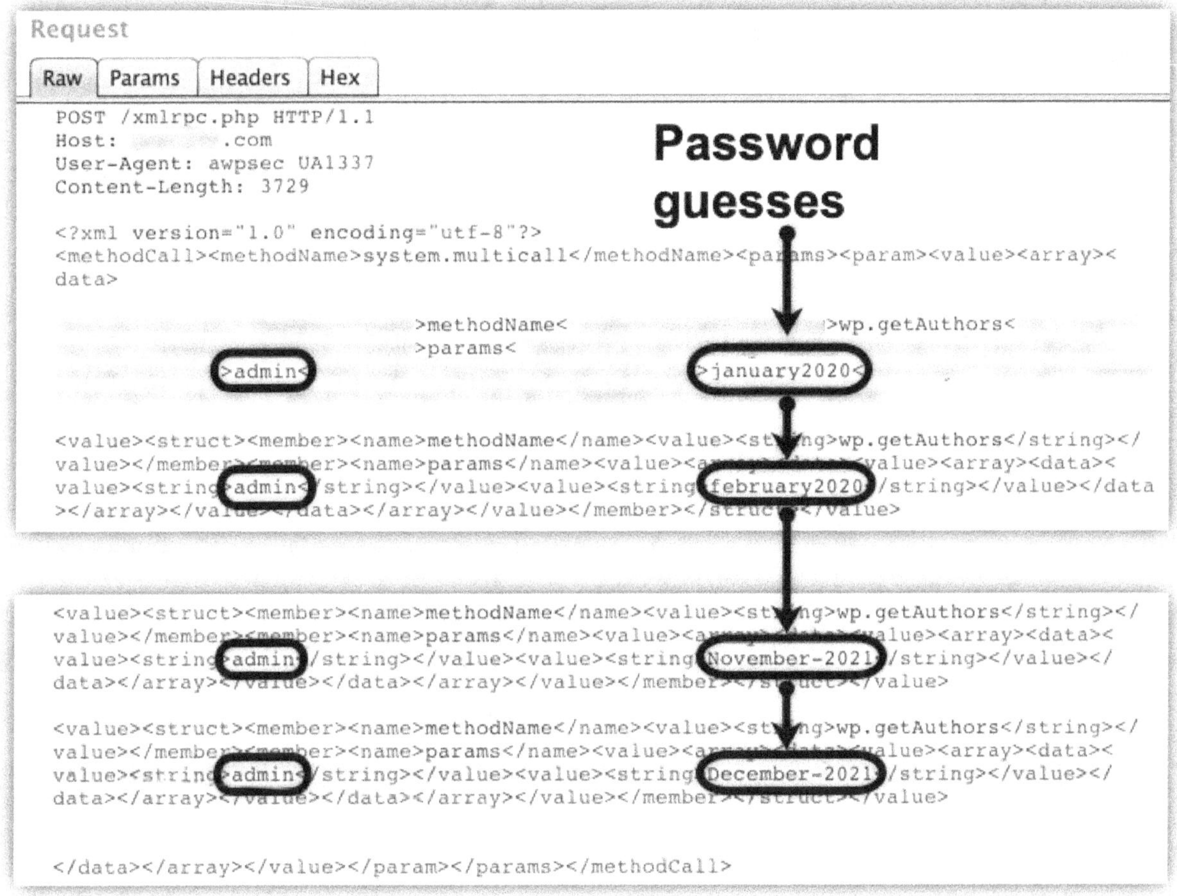

In Figure 5-4 the attacker watches the responses where the **faultCode** of **403** and **faultString** value of **Incorrect username or password** isn't returned. The response is matched to the request in order to reveal the valid password for **admin**.

FIGURE 5-4 *Response containing the faultCode and faultString values*

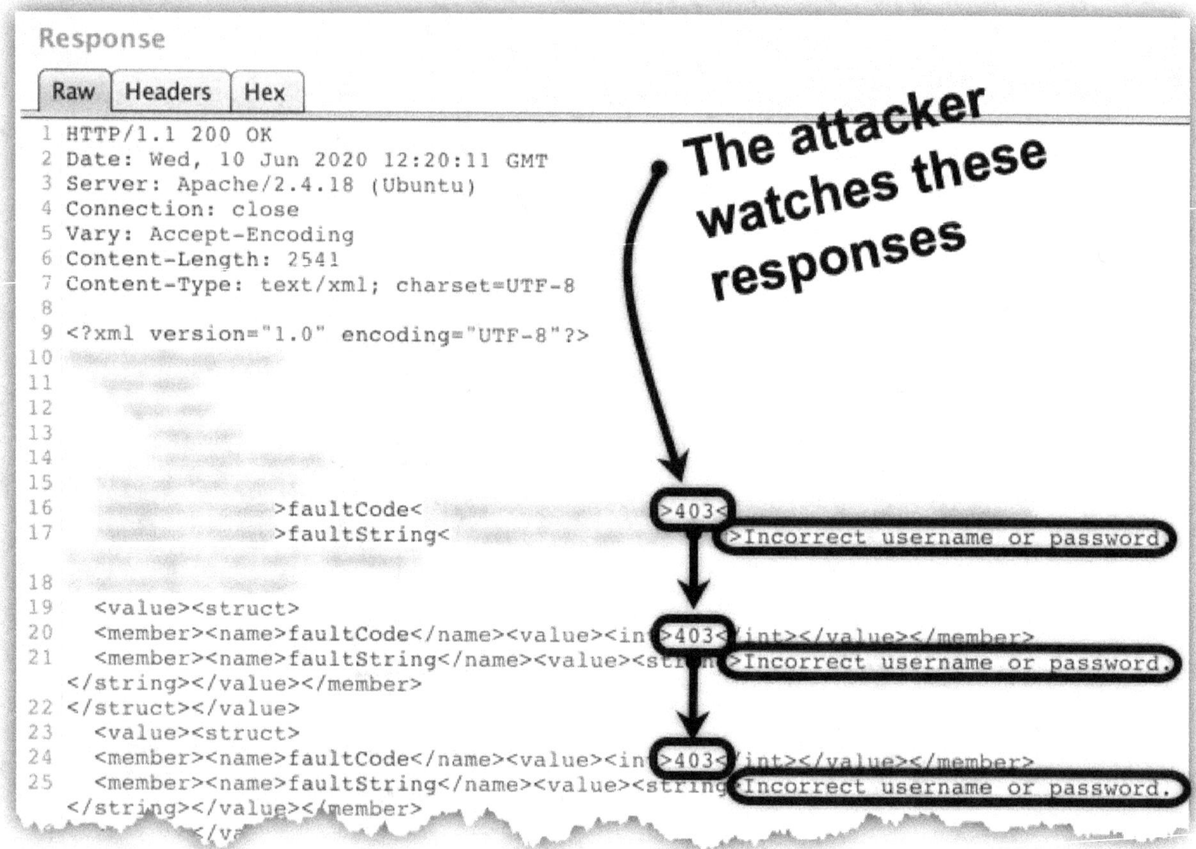

Your Apache access.log file shows a single entry per payload, even though the payload may contain 500 guesses.

```
210.16.189.4 - - [11/Jun/2020:10:53:37 +0000] "POST /xmlrpc.php HTTP/1.1" 200
3691 "-" "Apache-HttpClient/4.5.2 (Java/1.8.0_201)"
```

Advanced Solution

Dish out a little payback! If you disable XML-RPC entirely, it will cause issues with plugins and other functionality that you might not be aware of. Breaking your own site is never a good solution. A better solution is to modify the **system.multicall** method to ALWAYS RETURN A 403 ERROR and leave the rest of XML-RPC intact. The attacker will waste time because it looks like his payload is functioning correctly. Even if the attacker guesses a password correctly, he won't know it because you returned a 403 to him.

The system.multicall method lives in the PHP file named **class-IXR-server.php** in the **wp-includes/IXR** subfolder folder (e.g. /var/www/html/wp-includes/IXR). You will be modifying PHP code, so before you start making changes make a backup the file. If something goes wrong, you can return to normal. Use the **cp** command to copy the class-IXR-server.php file to something else, like class-IXR-server-**backup**.php.

```
cp class-IXR-server.php class-IXR-server-backup.php
```

Open up the file for editing using nano (or vim if you prefer).

```
nano class-IXR-server.php
```

Look for **function multiCall** toward the bottom of the file. In my version, it is the last function in the file. Here is the original code (or close to it), that you will be modifying.

```
function multiCall($methodcalls)
    {
```

```php
        // See http://www.xmlrpc.com/discuss/msgReader$1208
        $return = array();
        foreach ($methodcalls as $call) {
            $method = $call['methodName'];
            $params = $call['params'];
            if ($method == 'system.multicall') {
                $result = new IXR_Error(-32600, 'Recursive calls to
system.multicall are forbidden');
            } else {
                $result = $this->call($method, $params);
            }
            if (is_a($result, 'IXR_Error')) {
                $return[] = array(
                    'faultCode' => $result->code,
                    'faultString' => $result->message
                );
            } else {
                $return[] = array($result);
            }
        }
        return $return;
    }
```

This is what you want the function to look like when you are finished. To be clear, this isn't the whole file, just the multiCall function. Leave all of the other functions alone.

```php
    function multiCall($methodcalls)
    {
```

```
    // Modified by Grant Stokley

    $return = array();

    foreach ($methodcalls as $call) {

        $return[] = array(

            'faultCode' => '403',

            'faultString' => 'Incorrect username or password.'

        );

    }

    return $return;

}
```

To get there, start by removing these lines that are not **bold**.

```
function multiCall($methodcalls)

    {

        // See http://www.xmlrpc.com/discuss/msgReader$1208

        $return = array();

        foreach ($methodcalls as $call) {

            $method = $call['methodName'];

            $params = $call['params'];

            if ($method == 'system.multicall') {

                $result = new IXR_Error(-32600, 'Recursive calls to
system.multicall are forbidden');

            } else {

                $result = $this->call($method, $params);

            }

            if (is_a($result, 'IXR_Error')) {

                $return[] = array(
```

```
                'faultCode' => $result->code,
                'faultString' => $result->message
            );
        } else {
            $return[] = array($result);
        }
    }
    return $return;
}
```

That leave you with this…

```
function multiCall($methodcalls)
    {
        // See http://www.xmlrpc.com/discuss/msgReader$1208
        $return = array();
        foreach ($methodcalls as $call) {
            $return[] = array(
                'faultCode' => $result->code,
                'faultString' => $result->message
            );
        }
        return $return;
    }
```

From here notice the two lines that are most indented and start with **'fault**. That's what you will be modifying. Change the faultCode line from this…

```
'faultCode' => $result->code,
```

To this (the trailing coma is important)…

```
'faultCode' => '403',
```

Now change the faultString line from this…

```
'faultString' => $result->message
```

To this…

```
'faultString' => 'Incorrect username or password.'
```

That's the end of the required modifications. If you want to tidy up. Feel free to remove the extra indentation from the four lines inside the foreach loop and change the comment line to mention that this was modified by you. If everything went well your multiCall function should look like this

```
function multiCall($methodcalls)
{
    // Modified by Grant Stokley
    $return = array();
    foreach ($methodcalls as $call) {
        $return[] = array(
```

```
            'faultCode' => '403',
            'faultString' => 'Incorrect username or password.'
        );
    }
    return $return;
}
```

Go ahead a save (Ctrl+o) and exit (Ctrl+x) nano. The next step is to verify your site is still functioning properly.

Summary

XML-RPC is the method of choice for brute forcing passwords in WordPress. Using a PHP modification, you are able to deceive the attacker and tell him that all of his password guesses in the system.mutlicall payload are wrong, even if he may have had a correct one.

Chapter 6 | Disable Plugin Editor

Overview

The intent of the Plugin Editor (Figure 6-1) is to allow a convenient way for an administrator to edit files directly from the WordPress Dashboard. This would typically only be used by a very small percentage of WordPress admins, since it required an understanding of PHP, JavaScript, CSS, etc. The typical WordPress user enjoys not needing to know or understand any programming or scripting languages at all. Developers aren't going to use the Plugin Editor in any meaningful way, because it lacks a lot of the developer tools that you get in a proper IDE (Integrated Development Environment).

FIGURE 6-1 *Plugin Editor*

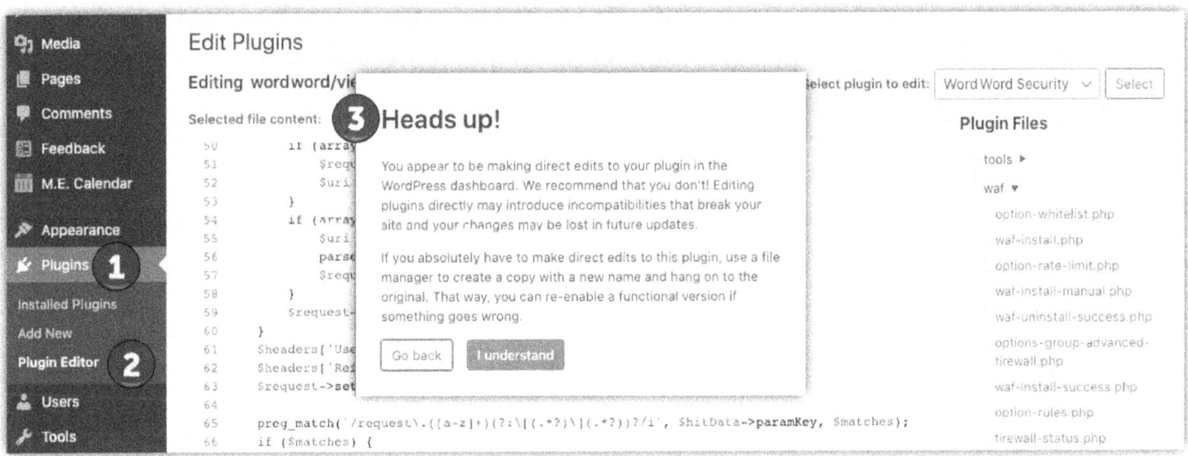

You know who does use it? The attacker does! All the attacker has to do is gain access to the dashboard and they have direct access to drop in any malicious code they want. There are several reasons why they want to run code on your site, a few examples.

- Host phishing pages for other targeted victims.
- Hosting spam pages on your site.
- Add spam links into your site.
- Send spam emails directly from your site, if you have a SMTP server configured.
- Attack other WordPress sites from your site.
- Redirect your entire site, to another website that they control.
- Defacement.
- Cryptocurrency mining.

The argument can be made, that if the attacker has administrator credentials to your WordPress website, you have more problems than just code being dropped in. While this is true, you want to minimize what they are able to do.

A novice attacker will blow up your posts, comments, and pages with blatantly obvious spam and hundreds of links to other unwanted garbage sites. A skilled attacker will not be as overt. They will stay quiet, harvest credentials of the other users of your site. Mine for cryptocurrency by using some of your resources during non-peak times. The only indicator that this is happening, is an increase in your hosting bill because your server had its CPUs cranking away when you weren't looking.

Disable the Plugin Editor

This is an easy one-liner configuration change. However, you must edit your **wp-config.php** file.

1. Locate your wp-config.php in the root directory of your WordPress Installation.
2. Use your file editor of choice and insert `define('DISALLOW_FILE_EDIT', true);` in between the opening comments after `<?php` and the before the MySQL comments.
3. Save and exit the file editor.
4. Restart Apache, `sudo apache2ctl restart`
5. Verify in the Dashboard that Plugin Editor option is now disabled.

The wp-config.php should look something like Figure 6-2:

FIGURE 6-2 *Example of wp-config.php*

```
  GNU nano 2.5.3                                        File: wp-config.php

<?php
/**
 * The base configurations of the WordPress.
 *
 * This file has the following configurations: MySQL settings, Table Prefix,
 * Secret Keys, and ABSPATH. You can find more information by visiting
 * {@link http://codex.wordpress.org/Editing_wp-config.php Editing wp-config.php}
 * Codex page. You can get the MySQL settings from your web host.
 *
 * This file is used by the wp-config.php creation script during the
 * installation. You don't have to use the web site, you can just copy this file
 * to "wp-config.php" and fill in the values.
 *
 * @package WordPress
 */

// Added by Grant Stokley to disable Plugin Editor
define('DISALLOW_FILE_EDIT', true);

// ** MySQL settings - You can get this info from your web host ** //
```

Summary

By disabling the Plugin Editor, you make the job of the attacker more difficult. They will have to find another way to get their malicious code on your site. The time they spend trying to figure that out, buys you more time to respond.

Chapter 7 | Disable PHP Error Reporting

Overview

When you see a character hacking into something on TV, you never see them mistype a command which goes unnoticed until execution, have communication issues, or even troubleshoot the magical code that they just typed in on the fly from memory. It makes for a good show for non-technical people. But for the rest of us who continually hit the backspace key, have to google things, and visualize tossing the laptop out of the windows because something just doesn't make sense, then debugging and error reporting are our best friends.

The same is true for real world attackers when trying exploit code against your site. It doesn't go perfect every time. In fact, novice attackers just download existing exploits and trying them out without actually understanding the exploit code at all. You don't want to help them figure it out by giving them useful feedback from your site.

How to Disable Error Reporting

This is an easy one-liner configuration change. However, you must edit your **wp-config.php** file.

1. Locate your wp-config.php in the root directory of your WordPress Installation.
2. Use your file editor of choice and insert `error_reporting(0);` in between the opening comments after `<?php` and the before the MySQL comments like in Figure 7-1. If you disabled Plugin Editor from the previous chapter, just drop this line in right after that.
3. Save and exit the file editor.
4. Restart Apache, `sudo apache2ctl restart`

5. Verify you site still functions normally.

FIGURE 7-1 *Example of wp-config.php*

```
GNU nano 2.5.3                                    File: wp-config.php

<?php
/**
 * The base configuration for WordPress
 *
 * The wp-config.php creation script uses this file during the
 * installation. You don't have to use the web site, you can
 * copy this file to "wp-config.php" and fill in the values.
 *
 * This file contains the following configurations:
 *
 * * MySQL settings
 * * Secret keys
 * * Database table prefix
 * * ABSPATH
 *
 * @link https://codex.wordpress.org/Editing_wp-config.php
 *
 * @package WordPress
 */

// Added by Grant Stokley to disable Plugin Editor
define('DISALLOW_FILE_EDIT', true);

// Added by Grant Stokley to disable PHP Error Reporting
error_reporting(0);

// ** MySQL settings - You can get this info from your web host ** //
/** The name of the database for WordPress */
```

Summary

By not providing feedback to the attacker, they will have a difficult time figuring out why their exploit isn't working. While the attacker wastes time blindly trying different code modifications, you have more time to respond.

Chapter 8 | Move wp-config.php

Overview

This is an optional and highly debated topic. For me, it seems like a no brainer to move it from a default location to a non-default location. Even if it does nothing else other than making attacker scripts not function properly, because it's not where they thought it would be.

Exploit Example

For example, an attacker develops an exploit for the FartPuppy plugin and unleashes it on the Internet in search of WordPress sites with the FartPuppy plugin. This exploit bypasses authentication and the payload is scripted to read the wp-config.php in the root WordPress directory to harvest the MySQL database credentials for further exploitation. If your wp-config.php file isn't where the payload script thought it was, it fails to harvest your database credentials and your site survives the attack.

Move wp-config.php

WordPress will automatically look in the parent directory for the wp-config.php file. So literally, all you have to do is...

1. SSH into the server.
2. `cd /var/www/html` (WordPress root directory).
3. Move the file (`sudo mv wp-config.php ../wp-config.php`)
4. Restart Apache (`sudo apache2ctl restart`).
5. Verify the site still works. If site breaks, move it back & restart Apache.

Summary

Hopefully by now, you've noticed a theme in this book. I don't like defaults and I want you to change as many of them as you can. By doing so, you are reducing the risk that an automated attack will be successful at exploiting your site.

Chapter 9 | Don't use Admin as a Username

Overview

Without Multi-factor Authentication (MFA), the only things keeping the attackers from gaining access to you site are the username and password. Everyone knows that the default WordPress account with administrator privileges is named **admin**. You can check this yourself with a simple Google search for "default wordpress user." It returns about 169,000,000 results. Knowing that fact, the attackers only need to guess, brute force, or phish the password to gain access.

Already Using Admin?

If you are reading this after the fact, and you are already using admin, you have a few options depending on your comfort level (TABLE 9-1). You can…

- Change from the default user login name of **admin** to something other than that, like **spaceghost**. However, you will be making changes in MySQL.
- Keep the **admin** user, but make your password really long and complex, like more that 20 characters (uppercase, lowercase, numbers, and symbols). Use a password manager to store it so you don't have to remember it or type it.
- Add Multi-factor Authentication (MFA)

TABLE 9-1 *Steps to take depending on your comfort level*

Your comfort Level	Step 1	Step 2	Step 3
Beginner	Make really long password for admin	Add MFA	
Advanced	Change admin to new username spaceghost	Make really long password for spaceghost	Add MFA

Choice of Usernames

I made the example of the using the name **spaceghost** for the administrator account. Hopefully, when you read that, you instantly thought it was a weird choice of username. That's actually the point. Again, everyone knows the default administrator account is **admin**. If you change it, the attacker will try to guess your new administrator account name.

Human nature dictates that after admin, most common *next* usernames that people choose will be one of these:

- Your name (combinations using first name, last name, and/or initials).
- Your company's name prepended to admin (e.g. acmeadmin or acme-admin).
- The name of one of your children.
- Your spouse's name.
- Your pet's name.
- Your favorite sports team name.

All of those guesses could be made by someone using social media and open source intelligence sources to research you and your company. Not to mention the more obvious source, the WordPress website itself. If you have any of that type of info on your website, make sure it's not part of your new administrator account's name.

Changing the username

If you decide to change the administrator account to something other than admin, you need to connect to the mysql database. You can do this using your tool of choice, but for simplicity sake, just use SSH from the command prompt. Type **sudo mysql -ustimpy42r -p** at the command prompt. Obviously, swap out stimpy42r for your MySQL password. Notice that there is no space between the **-u** and the password.

```
sudo mysql -ustimpy42r -p


Enter password:
Welcome to the MySQL monitor.  Commands end with ; or \g.
Your MySQL connection id is 14455
Server version: 5.7.30-0ubuntu0.16.04.1 (Ubuntu)


Copyright (c) 2000, 2020, Oracle and/or its affiliates. All rights reserved.


Oracle is a registered trademark of Oracle Corporation and/or its
affiliates. Other names may be trademarks of their respective
owners.
```

```
Type 'help;' or '\h' for help. Type '\c' to clear the current input
statement.
```

After you connect, you will need to switch to the wordpress database by typing **use <your wp database name>;**. For example, mine is set to **database4wp**, so I type **use database4wp;** at the mysql> prompt to change it.

```
mysql> use database4wp;
Reading table information for completion of table and column names
You can turn off this feature to get a quicker startup with -A

Database changed
```

The table where the users are stored in WordPress is wp_users. In Figure 9-1 you can what fields are available, type **desc wp_users;** at the mysql> prompt

FIGURE 9-1 *Description of the wp-users table in MySQL*

```
mysql> desc wp_users;
+--------------------+---------------------+------+-----+---------------------+----------------+
| Field              | Type                | Null | Key | Default             | Extra          |
+--------------------+---------------------+------+-----+---------------------+----------------+
| ID                 | bigint(20) unsigned | NO   | PRI | NULL                | auto_increment |
| user_login         | varchar(60)         | NO   | MUL |                     |                |
| user_pass          | varchar(255)        | NO   |     |                     |                |
| user_nicename      | varchar(50)         | NO   | MUL |                     |                |
| user_email         | varchar(100)        | NO   | MUL |                     |                |
| user_url           | varchar(100)        | NO   |     |                     |                |
| user_registered    | datetime            | NO   |     | 0000-00-00 00:00:00 |                |
| user_activation_key| varchar(255)        | NO   |     |                     |                |
| user_status        | int(11)             | NO   |     | 0                   |                |
| display_name       | varchar(250)        | NO   |     |                     |                |
+--------------------+---------------------+------+-----+---------------------+----------------+
10 rows in set (0.00 sec)
```

Notice the field names **user_login** and **display_name**, we want to check those out. Type **select ID, user_login, display_name from wp_users;** at the mysql> prompt (Figure 9-2).

FIGURE 9-2 *Results returned from select statement*

```
mysql> select ID, user_login, display_name from wp_users;
+----+------------+--------------+
| ID | user_login | display_name |
+----+------------+--------------+
|  1 | admin      | Joe Super Doe |
|  2 | backups    | Backup User  |
+----+------------+--------------+
2 rows in set (0.00 sec)
```

The **admin** user in the **user_login** field is what we want to change. To make the change use the **update** command. Like in Figure 9-3, type **update wp_users SET user_login = 'spaceghost' WHERE ID = 1;** at the mysql> prompt.

FIGURE 9-3 *Update wp_users statement*

```
mysql> update wp_users SET user_login = 'spaceghost' WHERE ID = 1;
Query OK, 1 row affected (0.01 sec)
Rows matched: 1  Changed: 1  Warnings: 0

mysql>
```

Verify the name change by running the **select** command again (Figure 9-4).

FIGURE 9-4 *Results returned from select statement*

```
mysql> select ID, user_login, display_name from wp_users;
+----+------------+--------------+
| ID | user_login | display_name |
+----+------------+--------------+
|  1 | spaceghost | Joe Super Doe |
|  2 | backups    | Backup User   |
+----+------------+--------------+
2 rows in set (0.00 sec)
```

Make sure that the value in the **display_name** doesn't match or infer what the **user_login** value is. The **display_name** field is what is shown to the public for posts and comments. An example of this is the **backups** user. Notice that the fields are in fact different, but you could infer what the value of the **user_login** is.

From the display_name of **Backups User**, typical guesses by the attacker would be:

- backups_user
- backup_user
- backupsuser
- backupuser
- **backups ←Correct Guess**
- backup
- buser

As you can see, in just a few guesses an attacker could infer the correct **user_login** value of **backups**. You should change the **display_name** to make this more difficult. Like in Figure 9-5, give it a more deceptive name of **Test User** for the **display_name**. Run the update on ID = 2 this time.

FIGURE 9-5 *Update wp_users statement*

```
mysql> update wp_users SET display_name = 'Test User' WHERE ID = 2;
Query OK, 1 row affected (0.01 sec)
Rows matched: 1  Changed: 1  Warnings: 0

mysql>
```

Verify the name change by running the **select** command again (Figure 9-6).

FIGURE 9-6 *Results returned from select statement*

```
mysql> select ID, user_login, display_name from wp_users;
+----+------------+---------------+
| ID | user_login | display_name  |
+----+------------+---------------+
|  1 | spaceghost | Joe Super Doe |
|  2 | backups    | Test User     |
+----+------------+---------------+
2 rows in set (0.00 sec)
```

The next attacker that comes along, attempts to guess what the user_login is based on the display_name found, just like the previous attacker. But this time the attacker is basing his guesses using **Test User** which is the deceptive description. His best guesses would be something like…

- test_user
- testuser

- t_user
- tester
- tuser
- testu

The attacker can use any combination of those two words, but all would be incorrect.

Summary

By choosing username that can't be derived from social engineering, the attacker will have to guess or brute force usernames and password combinations together, not just the password itself. This is exponentially harder to achieve.

Chapter 10 | Deny User-Agent Strings

Overview

I'm a North Korean attacker! Your company has geo-blocked all countries outside of the United States. My next move is to spin up a Kali Linux machine in an AWS Region that is inside of the United States. From there, I can bypass your geo-blocking restrictions. I get away it with until you finally analyze your logs and ask yourself, "how and why is a Mac browsing my site from inside AWS address space?" The answer is, there isn't a legitimate reason for that to happen. AWS typically contains servers only.

User-Agent String

When your web browser makes a request to a web server, it passes along information in the headers about your browser and the machine it's running on (Figure 10-1). This information is used by the server to make a number of decisions such as:

- Should the server return the mobile version of site or the desktop version?
- Are you using an outdated or unsupported browser? If so, return a message to user to update or use a supported browser instead.
- Do you have your company's custom User-Agent string that sends you to the development environment instead of the production site?
- Are you a web spider, bot, or human?

FIGURE 10-1 *User-Agent string*

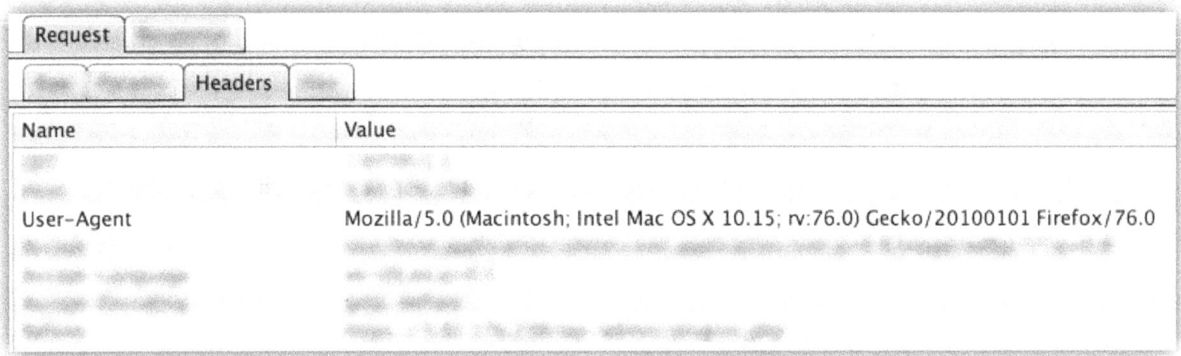

How to use it for Security

You can allow access based on such factors as the clients User-Agent string, Referer, and other HTTP request header fields. I have used them as an additional password field. It's not really a secret password, since anyone with a Man-In-The-Middle position can intercept it. However, it can be another factor that must be overcome by an attacker trying to gain access.

Access control, based on User-Agent strings, can be used to deny non-human requesters such as bots, curl, python, etc. access to some areas of the website or the entire site. Or use a more active defense strategy. Redirect those User-Agent strings to a decoy login screen. Where they spend time credential spraying into a login page that always results in "login failed."

Example

I have a real user-agent string from my Mac using Firefox that looks like this, **"Mozilla/5.0 (Macintosh; Intel Mac OS X 10.15; rv:77.0) Gecko/20100101 Firefox/77.0"** which shows up in the /var/log/apache2/access.log file, here is one of the entries.

```
10.255.20.245 - - [07/Jun/2020:18:23:45 +0000] "POST /wp-admin/admin-
ajax.php?_fs_blog_admin=true HTTP/1.1" 200 792 "https://10.82.176.238/wp-
admin/admin.php?page=WordTools" "Mozilla/5.0 (Macintosh; Intel Mac OS X
10.15; rv:77.0) Gecko/20100101 Firefox/77.0"
```

In Figure 10-2, I used Burp Suite Pro to replace my normal User-Agent string with this,
"Attacker User Agent 1337"

FIGURE 10-2 *Replace the User-Agent string*

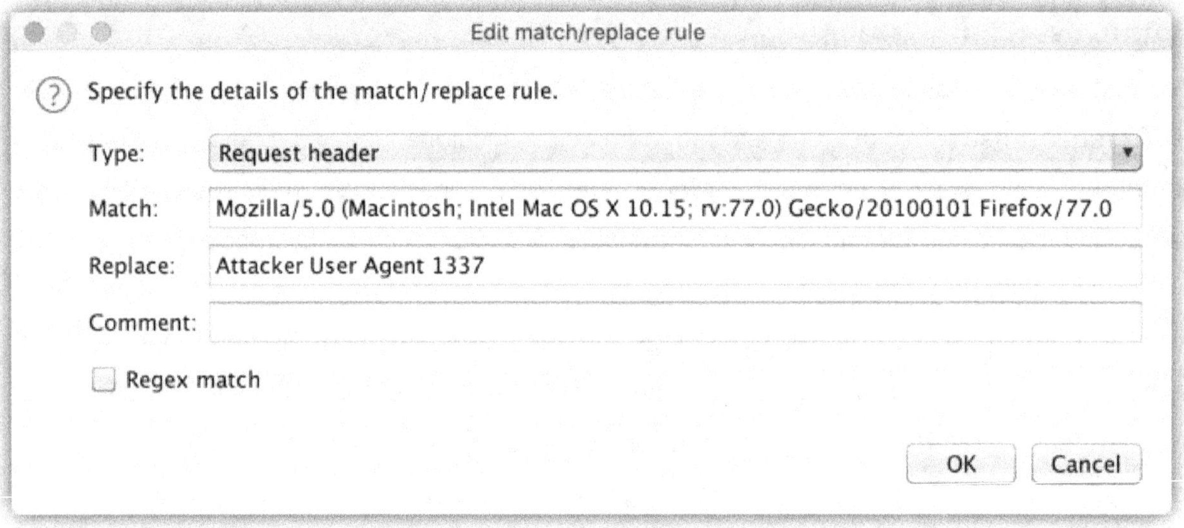

I save that replace rule and submit another request to the target WordPress site. Looking in the
log again, the user-agent string is indeed "Attacker User Agent 1337".

```
10.255.20.245 - - [07/Jun/2020:18:26:44 +0000] "GET /wp-
content/themes/vantage/images/retina/gallery-next.png HTTP/1.1" 200 905
"https://10.82.176.238/wp-content/themes/vantage/style.css?ver=1.14.5"
"Attacker User Agent 1337"
```

I edit my apache2.conf file using the **SetEnvIfNoCase** directive adding in a variable named **evil** with the exact string that I want to deny.

```
<Directory /var/www/html/ >
        AllowOverride None
        SetEnvIfNoCase User-Agent 'Attacker User Agent 1337' evil
        Order Deny,Allow
        Deny from env=evil
</Directory>
```

I restart apache, so it takes effect and make another request using the "Attacker User Agent String 1337" from my browser and get denied this time (Figure 10-3).

FIGURE 10-3 *Denied access based on User-Agent string*

Checking the log again, you can see that the request received a 403 Forbidden response from the server.

```
10.255.20.245 - - [07/Jun/2020:19:02:05 +0000] "GET /?page_id=3158 HTTP/1.1"
403 6362 "https://10.82.176.238/?page_id=3384" "Attacker User Agent 1337"
```

You can also use wildcards for that string value, otherwise it wouldn't be worth the effort since there is currently over 32 million active user-agent strings known to be in the wild. The wildcard uses a star (*) but requires a preceding dot (.) before the star on the front of the string but not the trailing one like, **.*anotherbadguy*** Also, simply add other bad user-agent strings to the list, like so…

```
<Directory /var/www/html/ >

     SetEnvIfNoCase User-Agent 'Attacker User Agent 1337' evil

     SetEnvIfNoCase User-Agent .*anotherbadguy* evil

     SetEnvIfNoCase User-Agent .*Bot* evil

     ...
```

Summary

You now have another weapon in which to defend your site. User-agent strings can of course be spoofed, like I just did in the example. However, you will be able to weed out non-human bad actors like botnets, spiders, etc.

Chapter 11 | CAPTCHA

Overview

CAPTCHA is an acronym for **C**ompletely **A**utomated **P**ublic **T**uring test to tell **C**omputers and **H**umans **A**part. CAPTCHAs are those annoying puzzles that you must solve in order to do certain tasks, such as login (Figure 11-1). The intention of them is to identify what is human and what it not. Then only allow the humans access to the site.

Figure 11-1 *Example of CAPTCHAs*

Attackers Bypass the CAPTCHAs

Not only is it a stupid acronym, but there are many services and tools out there that automate the bypassing of the CAPTCHAs (Figure 11-2). Attackers use the APIs provided by these services to bypass the CAPTCHAs and continue their automated attacks. Leaving legit human users behind playing the annoying games rather than getting any value from your site.

Honestly, if a search result brings me to a site containing a CAPTCHA, I immediately return to the search results and try the next site.

FIGURE 11-2 *Example CAPTCHA solving services on the Internet*

Summary

Don't Use CAPTCHAs! The negative user experience outweighs the perceived security value. CAPTCHAs just cause user friction and doesn't stop an attacker who has targeted your site.

You are supposed to be securing the WordPress site, not pushing user away from it. That's what CAPTCHAs do!

Chapter 12 | Identify Risky Plugins

Overview

Currently there are over 56,000 possible plugins that you can install on your WordPress site (Figure 12-1). I'll show you how to avoid the risky ones. Unfortunately, not all plugin developers are created equal. Creating a plugin is relatively easy with only mild skills in PHP. This is one of the reasons WordPress is so popular. Spend a weekend on YouTube watching videos and you can learn to develop working PHP code. Some plugins are developed by people doing exactly that. They developed a plugin to do a particular function on their own site and decided to share it with the world. Then moved on to something else without sticking around to secure it or even maintaining it. If you install one of these plugins, you could be in for a surprise down the road.

Narrowing the Field

From a security standpoint, each plugin and theme that you install adds to the attack surface. However, I highly recommend that you install a 2FA plugin! The trick is only installing secure and well written plugins and themes. I'll show you how to locate possible 2FA plugin candidates. Go to **wordpress.org/plugins/** from your browser (Figure 12-1). Alternatively, if you are already logged into your WordPress site, you can open up your dashboard, click **Plugins**, then click the **Add New**. Both methods provide you with a search box.

FIGURE 12-1 Plugins page on *wordpress.org*

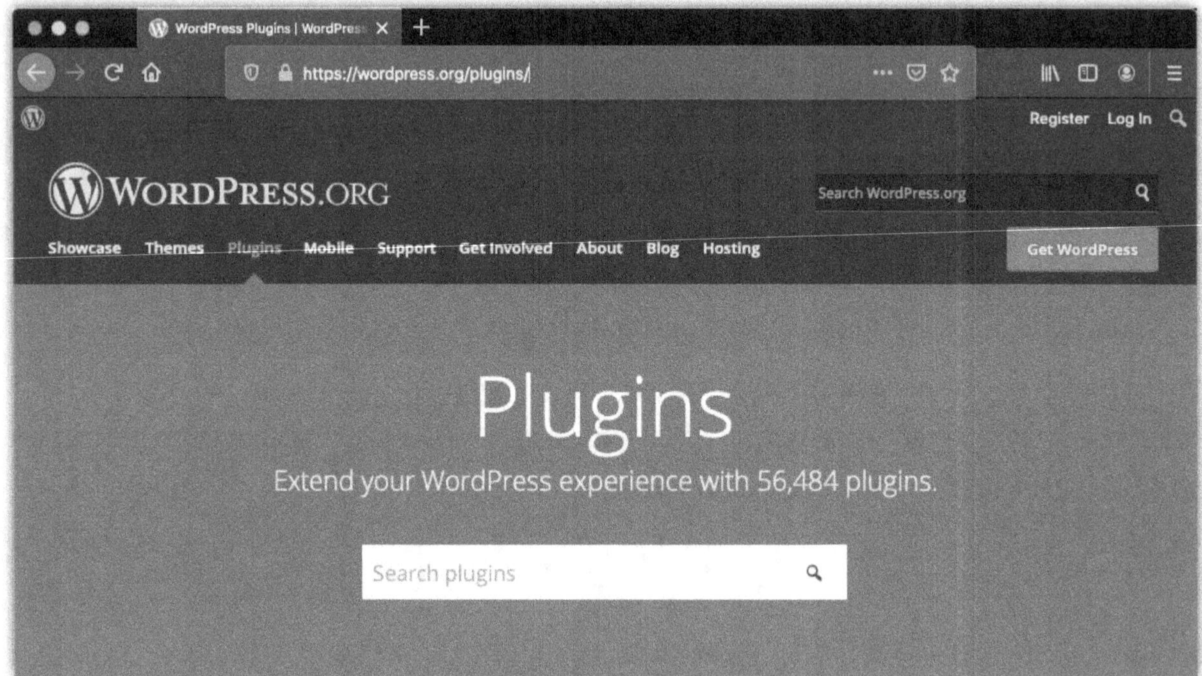

Since we are interested in security, let's see what security related plugins are available. Type **security** into the search box and press return. You will see too many pages of results to sift through. Security is too vague, lets change the search to **2fa** and press return. You should get three or four pages of results back, which is more manageable. Figure 12-2 shows how to identify the attributes for each plugin. To narrow the field, the initial things that to look for are:

- Active installation count = highest
- The plugin has been tested with the current version of WordPress
- The number of reviews = highest

- Ratings >= 4 stars

FIGURE 12-2 *Plugin attributes*

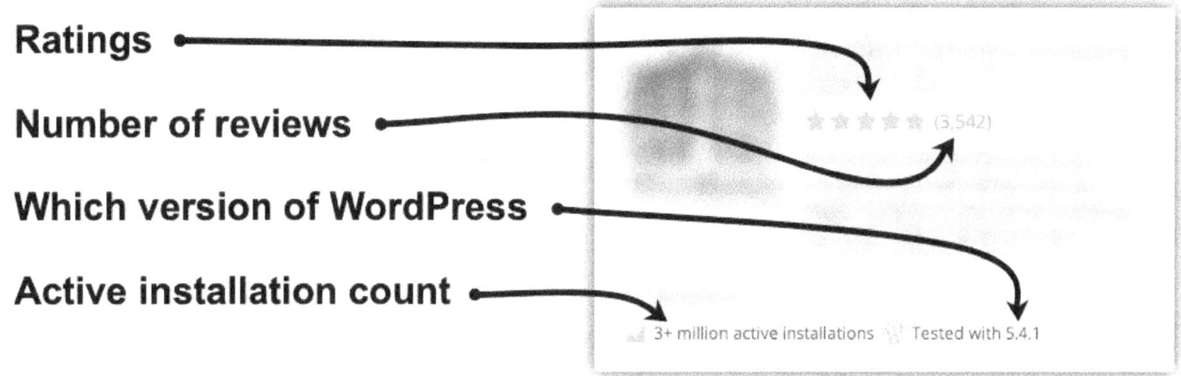

Figure 12-3 shows the first page of results for plugins that contain 2fa in the title or description. Immediately there is a distinction between the plugins. Wordfence has 3+ million active installations, has a 5-star rating with 3,542 reviews (more than all of the other plugins combined), and it has been tested on the current version (5.4.1 at the time).

FIGURE 12-3 *Comparing Wordfence to the other plugins*

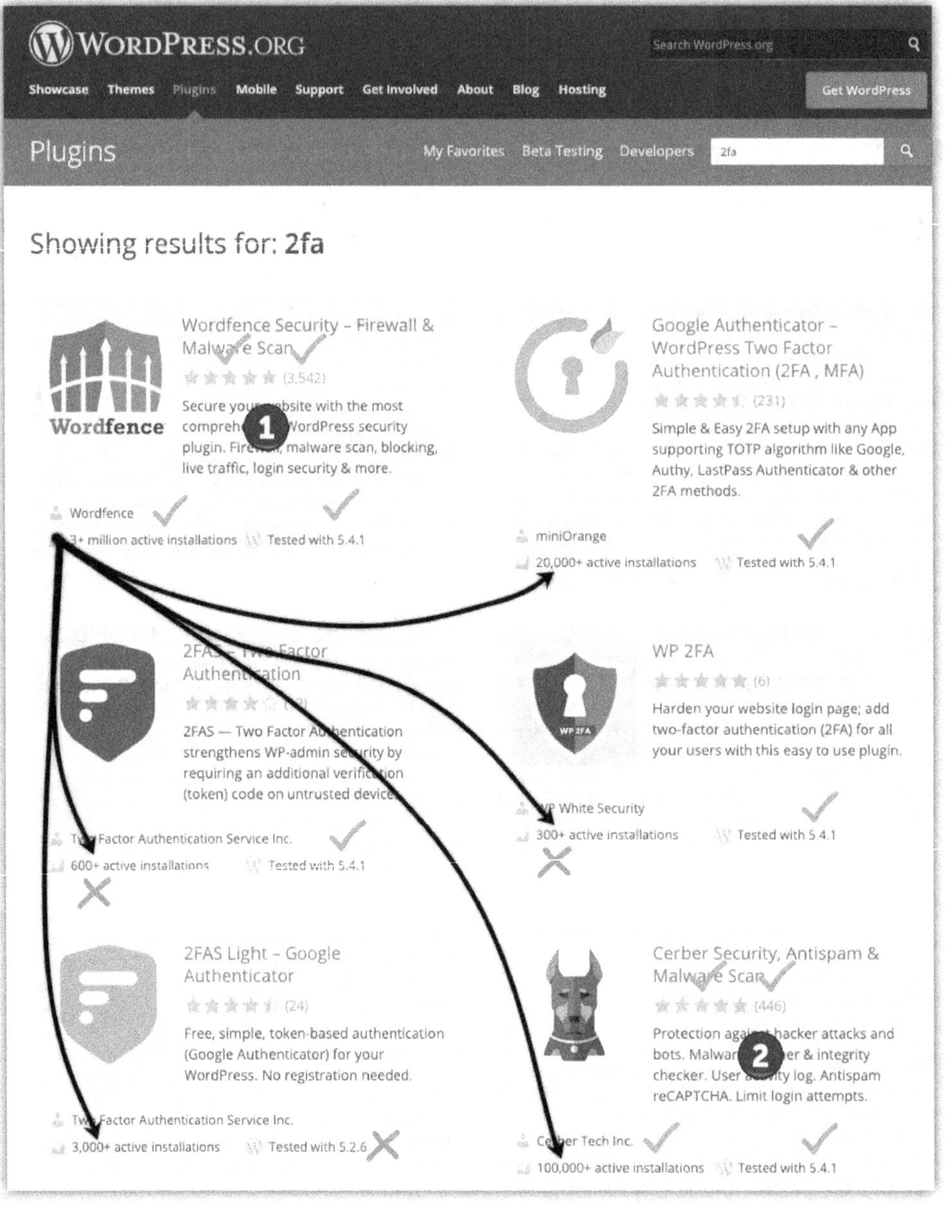

The Wordfence plugin looks like the clear choice. However, let's dig into it further to verify. If it's missing features, has fake reviews, or anything else that we don't like, then move on to the second choice.

The second choice would be the Cerber Security, Antispam & Malware Scan plugin since it has over 100,000 active installations, has a 5-star rating with 446 reviews, and was also tested in the current version of WordPress.

Not Choosing a Plugin

There are a few factors that you can use to eliminate plugins from your list of candidates.

- Bad or no developer reputation.
- Low frequency of updates.
- Not tested on current version of WordPress.
- Reviews look fake.

You can't always believe the reviews and comments since these can be faked. A few indicators that the reviews are fake:

- There are a lot of comments, but most of them are one-liners and generic.
- The ratio of reviews to active installations is way too high (Figure 12-4). A rule of thumb is that usually less than 1 out of 100 people will actually leave a review (1/100th). For example, look at the **Google Authenticator – WordPress Two Factor Authentication (2FA, MFA)** plugin. It has 200,000+ active installations with 231 reviews, which is closer to 1/1000th.

- The frequency of reviews is high very early in the release of the plugin. In other words, the reviews are too close together, timewise, to be real.

FIGURE 12-4 *Example of a plugin to skip over*

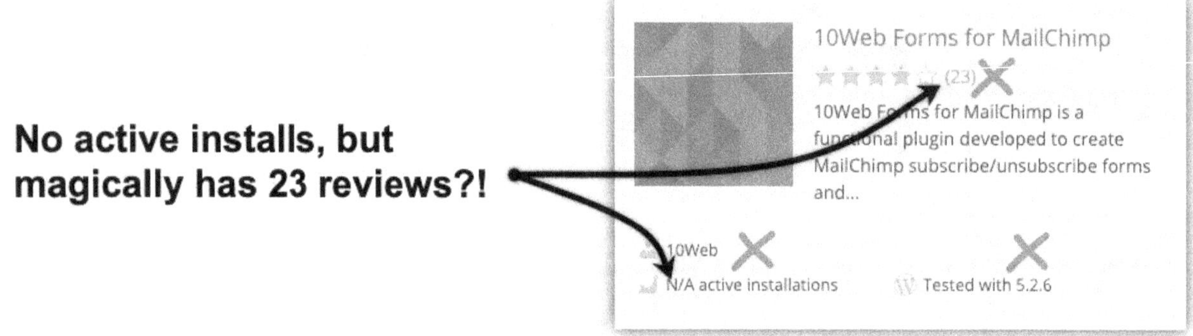

Plugin Vulnerabilities

A poorly written, abandoned, or malicious plugins are the #1 source of all vulnerabilities to a WordPress site. A well know collection of vulnerabilities for WordPress is **wpvulndb.com**. A report they published stated that 75% of all vulnerabilities came from the plugins, while 14% came from the WordPress code itself, and the remaining 11% came from installed themes.

Once you have narrowed down your plugin selection to a few candidates. You can use the **wpvulndb.com** site (Figure 12-5) to find the vulnerabilities that have been reported for those plugins.

FIGURE 12-5 *WordPress Plugin Vulnerabilities*

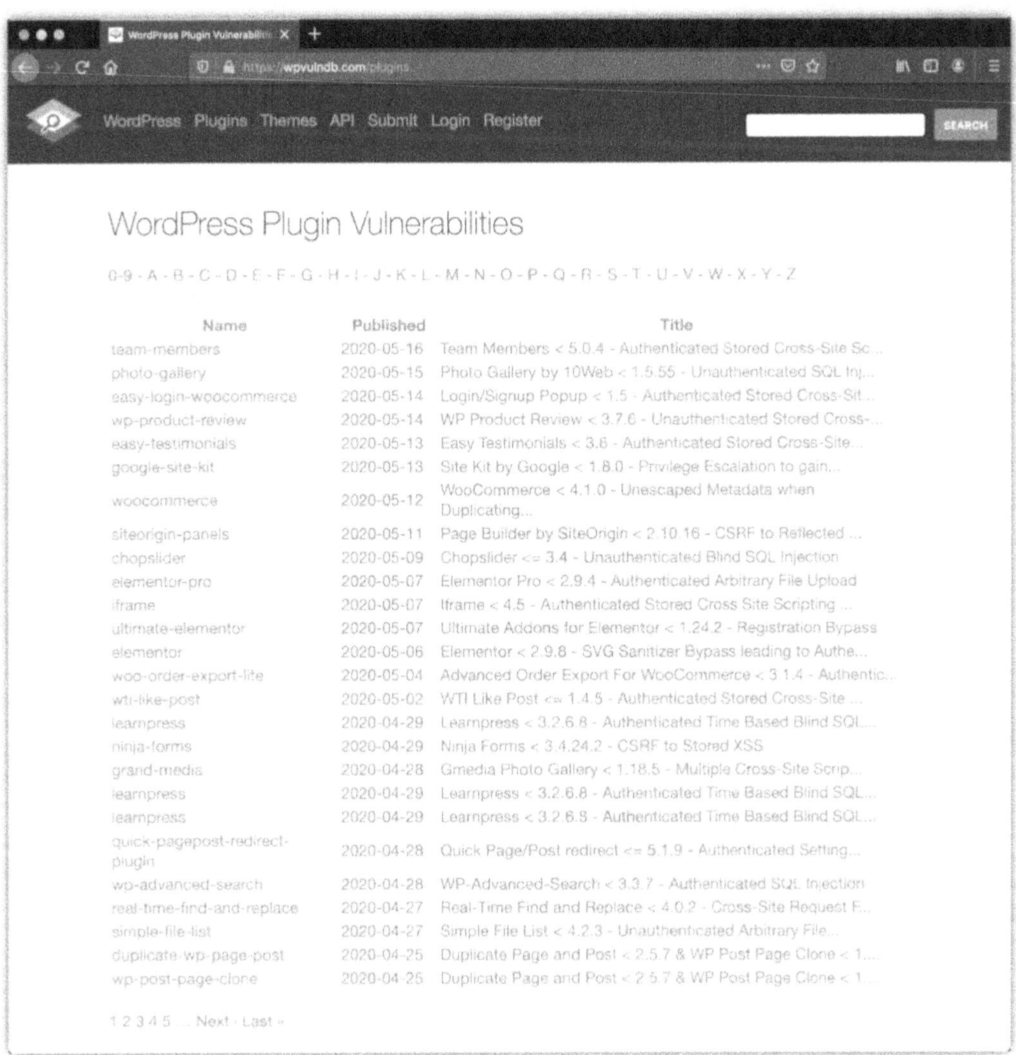

After navigating to **https://wpvulndb.com**, click **Plugins** in the header and that will show you a listing of the most recent vulnerabilities found for all known plugins. This list is vaguely searchable to make it a little easier to wade through the list of vulnerabilities. However, this doesn't always work well if the name isn't unique enough. For instance, we are looking for vulnerabilities in Wordfence. Figure 12-6 shows the results of searching for **wordfence**.

FIGURE 12-6 *Results of searching for wordfence*

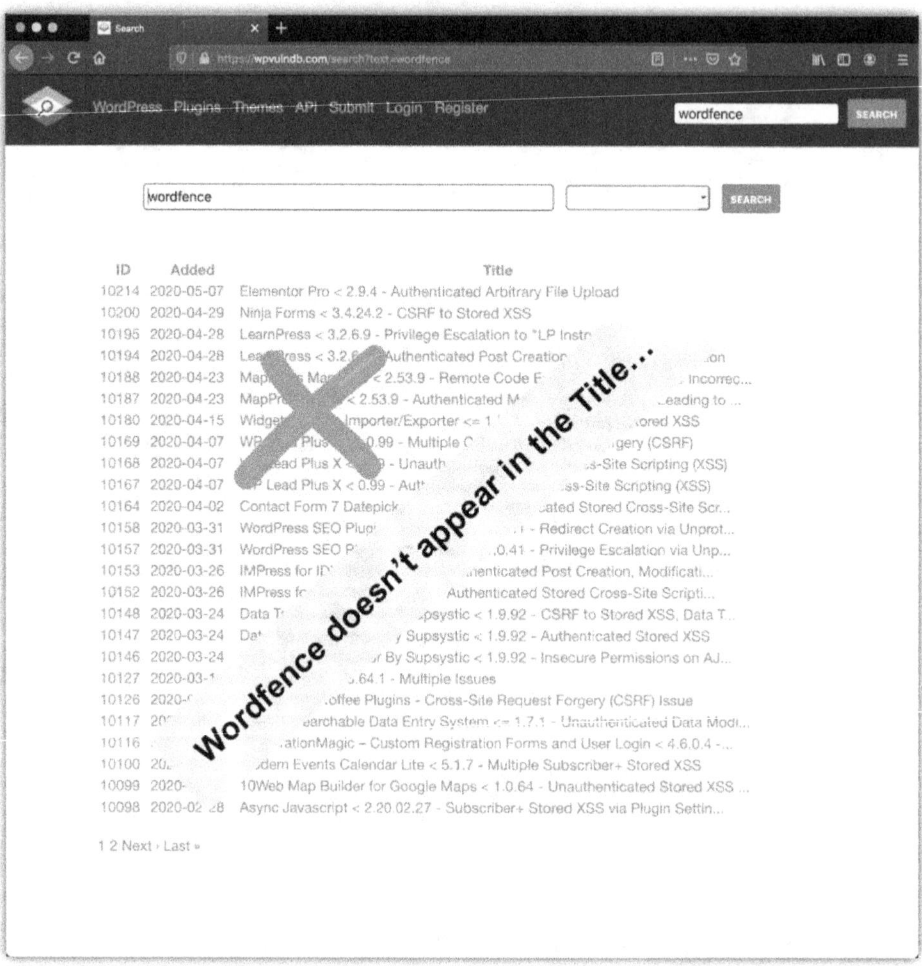

There are two pages of results when searching for **wordfence**, none of the results on the entire first page has Wordfence in the title, Interesting! You might be wondering (as I did) why they are even showing up in the results then? Clicking the first result shows us the details of that vulnerability.

FIGURE 12-7 *The Description and URL fields contains Wordfence*

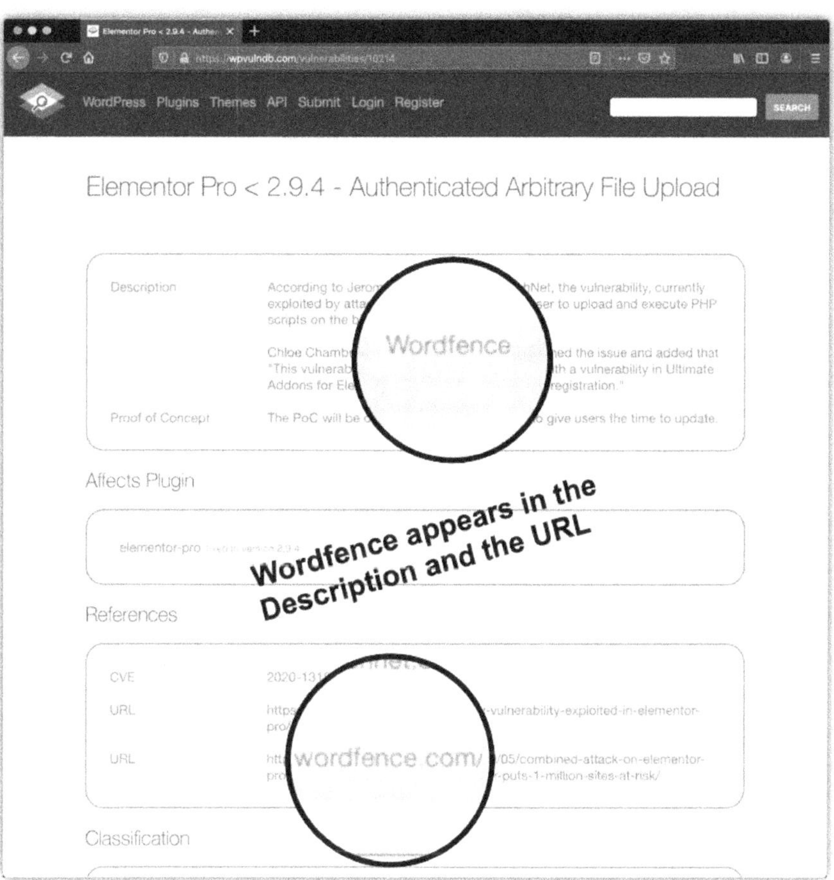

In Figure 12-7, you can see **Wordfence** is appearing in the description and URL fields. That's disappointing from a finding vulnerabilities standpoint, but this does make me feel even better about Wordfence since it appears, they are the one's finding vulnerabilities and reporting them.

If you are savvy with using API calls and parsing JSON then you can register with wpvulndb.com, get an API key, and make an API call to retrieve the array of vulnerabilities for a plugin. As an example, I called the API and retrieved only the **title**, **published_date**, **vuln_type** to make the results more legible.

```json
{
    "wordfence":{
        "friendly_name":"Wordfence Security - Firewall \u0026 Malware Scan",
        "latest_version":"7.4.7",
        "last_updated":"2020-04-23T16:38:00.000Z",
        "popular":true,
        "vulnerabilities":[
            {
                "title":"Wordfence 3.8.6 - lib/IPTraf.php User-Agent Header
Stored XSS",
                "published_date":"2014-08-01T10:58:38.000Z",
                "vuln_type":"XSS"
            },
            {
                "title":"Wordfence 3.8.1 - Password Creation Restriction Bypass",
                "published_date":"2014-08-01T10:58:38.000Z",
                "vuln_type":"AUTHBYPASS"
            },
```

```
        {
            "title":"Wordfence 3.8.1 - wp-admin/admin.php whois Parameter
Stored XSS",
            "published_date":"2014-08-01T10:58:39.000Z",
            "vuln_type":"XSS"
        },
        {
            "title":"Wordfence 3.3.5 - XSS \u0026 IAA",
            "published_date":"2014-08-01T10:58:39.000Z",
            "vuln_type":"MULTI"
        },
        {
            "title":"Wordfence 5.2.4 - Unspecified Issue",
            "published_date":"2014-09-22T18:47:58.000Z",
            "vuln_type":"UNKNOWN"
        },
        {
            "title":"Wordfence 5.2.4 - IPTraf.php URI Request Stored XSS",
            "published_date":"2014-09-22T18:52:28.000Z",
            "vuln_type":"XSS"
        },
        {
            "title":"Wordfence 5.2.3 - Banned IP Functionality Bypass",
            "published_date":"2014-09-22T19:33:44.000Z",
            "vuln_type":"BYPASS"
        },
        {
            "title":"Wordfence 5.2.3 - Multiple Vulnerabilities",
```

```json
        "published_date":"2014-09-27T12:37:39.000Z",
        "vuln_type":"MULTI"
      },
      {
        "title":"Wordfence <= 5.2.4 - Multiple Vulnerabilities (XSS &
Bypasses)",
        "published_date":"2014-10-07T16:26:43.000Z",
        "vuln_type":"MULTI"
      },
      {
        "title":"Wordfence 5.2.2 - XSS in Referer Header",
        "published_date":"2014-12-01T13:18:37.000Z",
        "vuln_type":"XSS"
      },
      {
        "title":"Wordfence <= 5.1.4 - Cross-Site Scripting (XSS)",
        "published_date":"2014-12-08T13:19:49.000Z",
        "vuln_type":"XSS"
      },
      {
        "title":"Wordfence <= 7.1.12 - Username Enumeration Prevention
Bypass",
        "published_date":"2018-10-02T00:00:00.000Z",
        "vuln_type":"BYPASS"
      }
    ]
  }
}
```

It appears that Wordfence had a several vulnerabilities with a **published_date** value between 2014 and 2018. Looking at the **last_updated** field, it shows a date of 2020-04-23. That makes me more confident that this is a secure plugin since that is pretty close to the date of this writing.

Static Application Security Testing (SAST) for Plugins

Static Application Security Testing (SAST) looks at the source code before execution. This is different from vulnerability scanning or Dynamic Application Security Testing (DAST), which scans the WordPress site and plugins while the server is up and running.

The developer(s) of the plugin *should* be performing SAST during their Software Development Lifecycle (SDLC) process. However, this is not always done by the developer. This is where you come in. You scan it before you install it! There are plenty of online free scanners that do this for you. A popular example is Code Risk at coderisk.com (Figure 12-8).

FIGURE 12-8 *Example of coderisk.com*

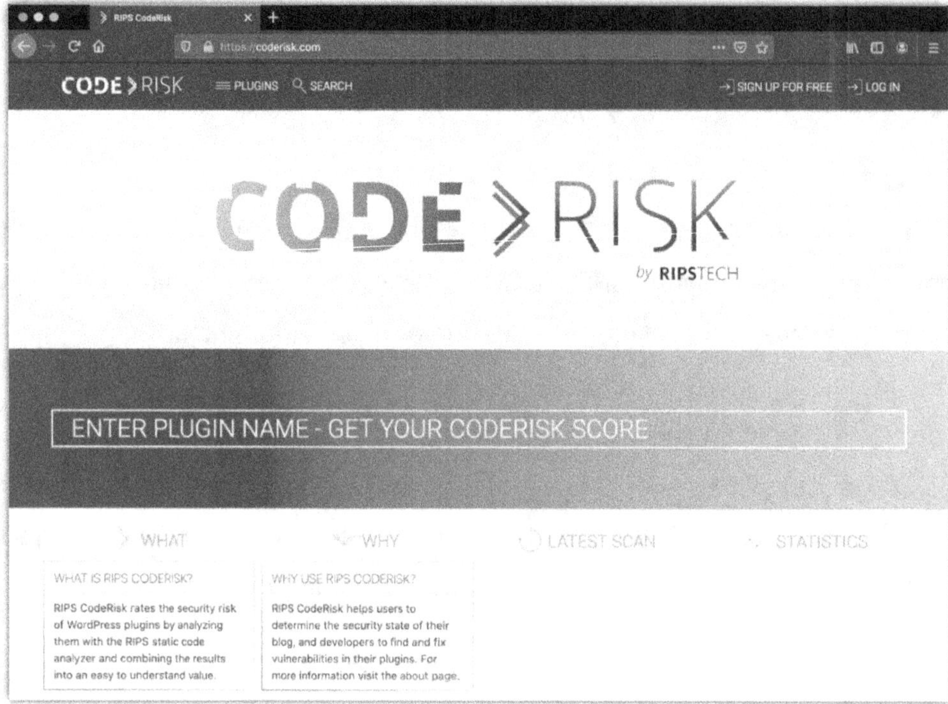

Start typing in the name of the plugin, like Wordfence for instance. It will return results as you are typing the search string. Clicking on **Wordfence Security – Firewall & Malware Scan** result pulls up the details of the scan.

FIGURE 12-9 *Code Risk score for Wordfence*

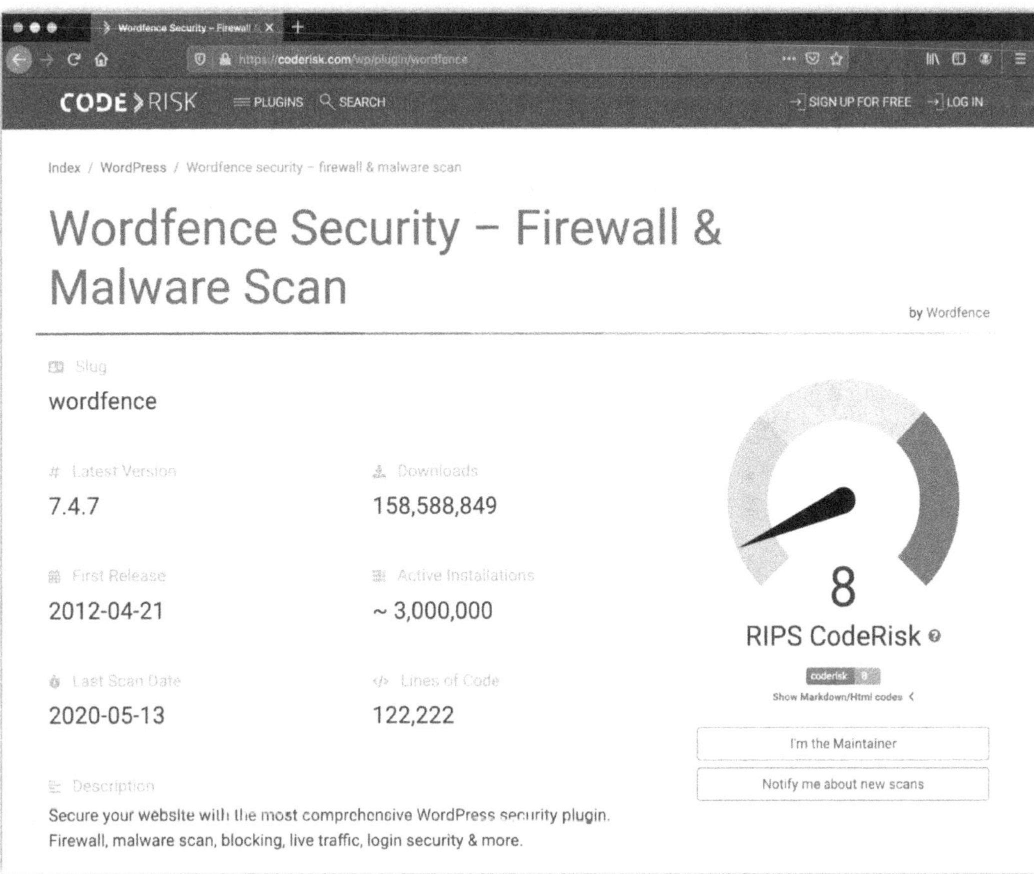

RIPS stands for **R**e-**I**nforced **P**rogramming **S**ecurity and the gauge in Figure 12-9 shows a RIPS CodeRisk score of 8. On this gauge, a risk score of 0 (green) means that this plugin is completely safe and a risk score of 100 (red) is an indicator of really vulnerable code.

By comparison our second choice didn't turn out so good. In Figure 12-10, the Cerber Security plugin has a risk score of 100. It doesn't get any worse than that.

FIGURE 12-10 *Code Risk score for wp-cerber*

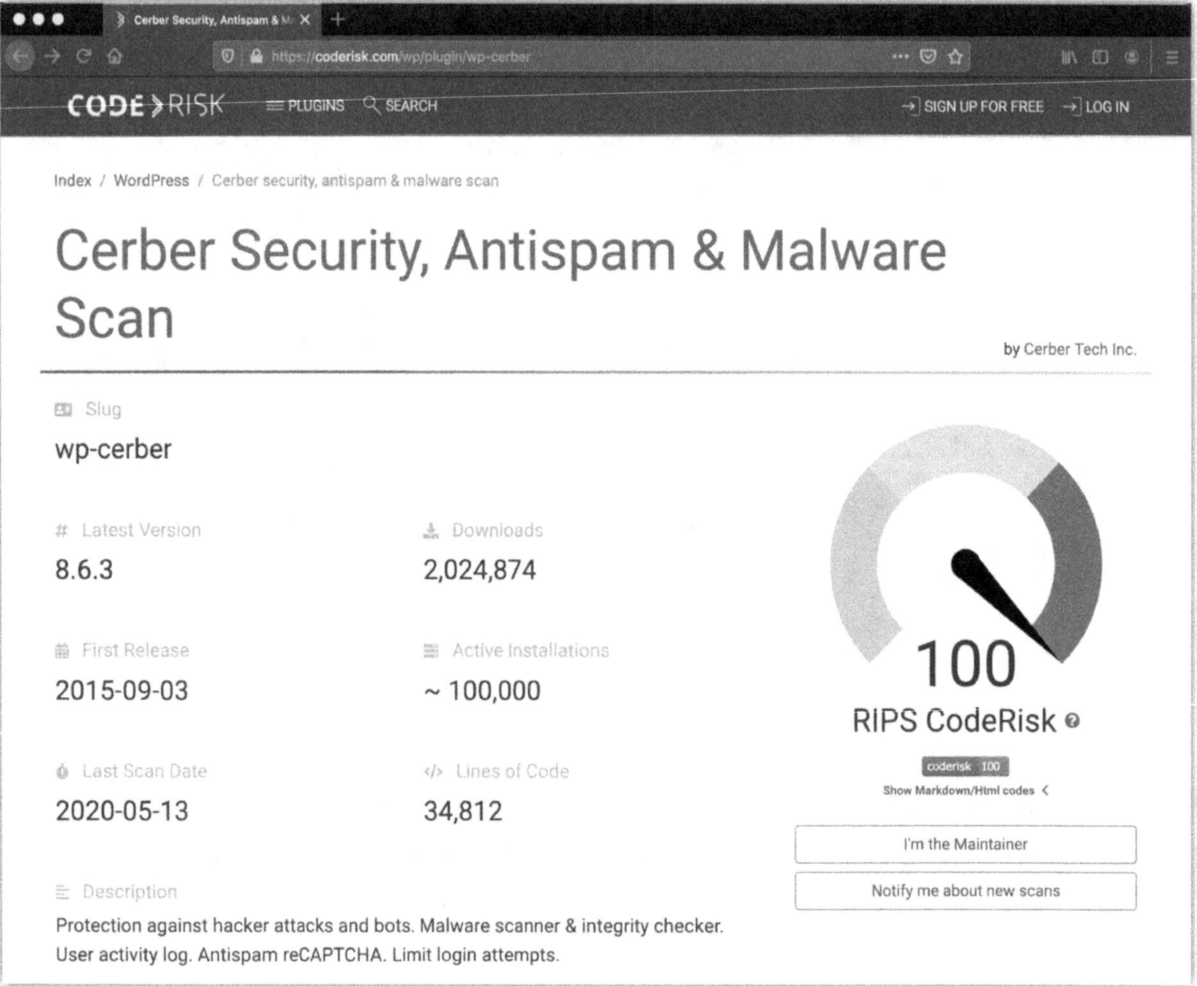

That is a perfect example of why you check into what you are installing, you don't want a poison plugin on your site!

Summary

Avoid plugins with low installation counts, has not been tested on the current version of WordPress, check the reviews and determine if they are too good to be true. Check your plugin candidate for vulnerabilities using wpvulndb.com. Finally, run a static code analysis against the plugin with a site like coderisk.com.

Chapter 13 | Install 2FA Plugin

Overview

You got phished! You typed your valid credentials into a fake WordPress login page without noticing. While you spend time retyping your password a few more times, the attacker has already logged into your site as you and changed your password. You are now locked out of your own site and attacker has full control. Now what?!...

Without 2FA, you will be restoring your site from backup. With 2FA, the attacker still harvests your valid credentials. However, this time after entering the username and password, he is given the 2FA Code request page (Figure 13-1). The attacker doesn't have the 2FA code and thus is denied access. Your site remains safe and buys you time to change your password.

FIGURE 13-1 *Prompt for 2FA Code*

The Factors

Two-Factor Authentication (aka 2FA) is sometimes called Multi-Factor Authentication (aka MFA). The factors that are being referred to are:

1. Something you **know**. This is your username and password combination.
2. Something you **have**. We will be adding a Time-based One-Time Password (aka TOTP) based authenticator application. The application produces an additional password that is always changing but is in sync with the authentication provider.
3. Something you **are**. Biometrics such as facial recognition, fingerprints, retina scans are used as an additional factor. This is what modern phones and laptops are using to log you in to the device.
4. Some**where** you are. Location can be used as an additional factor. Legal gambling sites are regulated to only allow gambling using a mobile application if the user is in a physical location where gambling is allowed by law. To acquire this factor the location services from the GPS are used.

A default WordPress installation is only using one factor, the username and password combination. It becomes 2FA when you require one of the other factors in addition to the username and password.

Time-Based Authentication for 2FA

You share a secret key with authenticating authority. Then at designated time increments, a value is computed using the key and an algorithm. If both parties started with the same key and the algorithm was applied to both of them the same number of times, then the value should be equal. If they are in fact equal, access is granted.

Figure 13-2 is a simple example of how this works. You and your WordPress server decide on a key of 1010 at a particular start time. The algorithm that both of you will use is simply adding 202 to the current value to get a new value. When the first time increment passes, 202 is added to 1010, and the new shared value is 1212 (e.g. 1010+202=1212). The same algorithm is applied at each time increment. So, after the algorithm has been applied to the key five times, you and your server both know that the value should be 2020.

FIGURE 13-2 *Simplified example of a time-based algorithm*

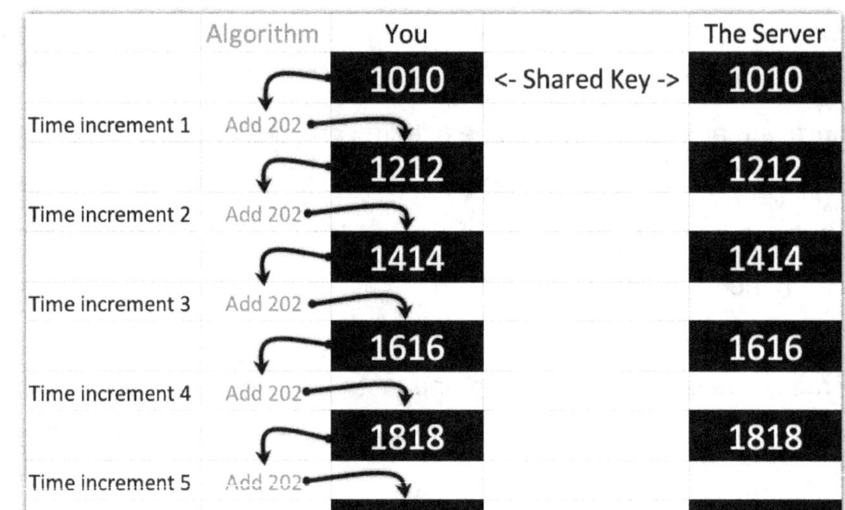

Installing 2FA

TOTP is the acronym for Time-based One-Time Password. You will need to install a TOTP authenticator application on your mobile phone in order to share a key, the algorithm, and agreed upon time increments between you and your server's carefully chosen 2FA plugin.

There are several authenticator applications out there. The more popular ones are Google Authenticator, Microsoft Authenticator, Duo, Authy, and LastPass Authenticator.

After installing the authenticator app on your phone, it's time to sync the two. This step will vary based on the actual software and plugin that you've chosen, but the concepts are pretty standard for all of them. 2FA will be added per user account, so each user that will be using 2FA will go through an individual setup process. During the setup process, the plugin will present you with a key. That key might be a QR code or sets of numbers. You will add that key your authenticator app, like in Figure 13-3.

FIGURE 13-3 *Add a key to your authenticator app*

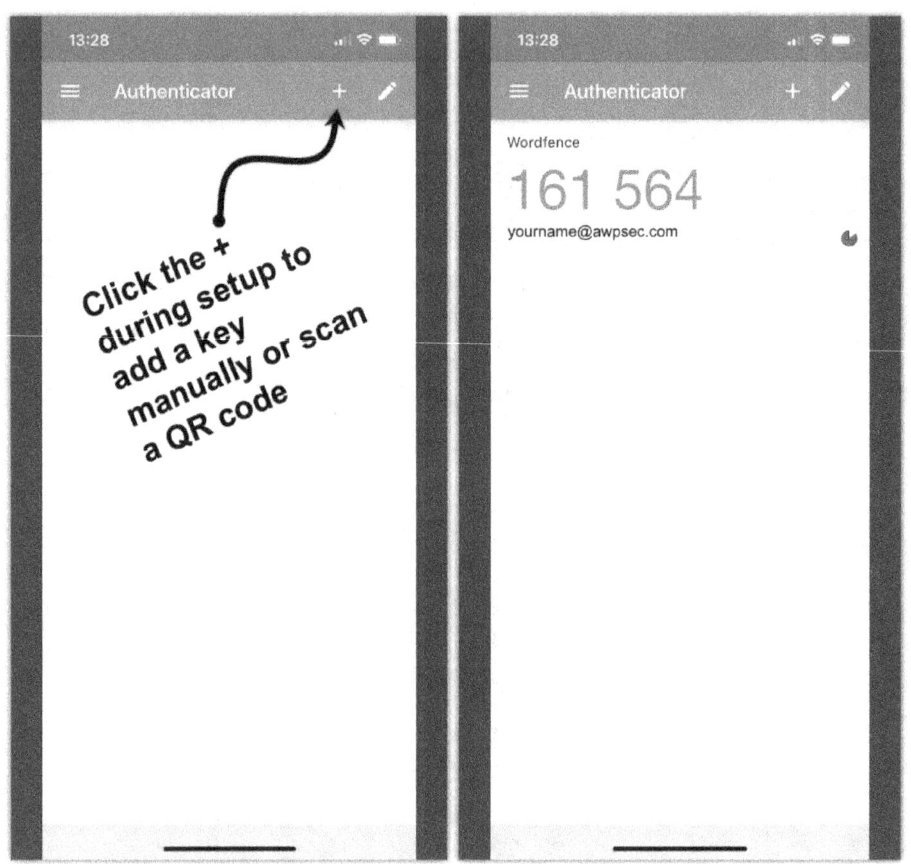

After successfully completing the setup process, the authenticator app will display digits that will change every 30 to 60 seconds. Those digits will be used as the 2nd Factor of Authentication after you have successfully entered your username and password combination on your WordPress site.

Summary

With the 2FA plugin up and running and requiring it for all administrator accounts, you have made the attacker's job much harder. Even with stolen credentials, the attacker is denied access since he is unable to provide the 2FA digits that are now required.

Chapter 14 | Logging

Overview

Security events are logged in several places such as the Apache, MySQL, and the operating system itself. You can't un-see the logs once you've seen them. Inevitably there are going to be entries in the logs that will alarm you, and you will want to take action. There will be evidence of past and ongoing attacks in those log files. With that information at hand, you can actively defend your site.

Apache Logs

Apache has two logs that you will want to keep an eye on.

- /var/log/apache2/**access.log**
- /var/log/apache2/**error.log**

Apache's access.log File

The access.log file, located in the /var/log/apache2/ directory, contains the IP addresses of everything making HTTP GET and POST requests to your server. You identify attacks from this file. Opening the access.log file you will see entries like these in Figure 14-1.

FIGURE 14-1 *Entries in the access.log file*

Here we have a single source IP address making rapid POST requests to xmlrpc.php. If you remember the XML-RPC chapter from earlier in the book, this is evidence that brute force attack took place.

Figure 14-2 is an example of a SQL Injection attack. Notice the **UNION**, **SELECT**, and **order by** commands in the query string.

FIGURE 14-2 *SQL Injection attack found in the access.log file*

Figure 14-3 shows several blind SQL Injection attempts with URL encoding in the query string. It's hard to understand what the attacker is trying to accomplish until you decode it.

FIGURE 14-3 *Blind SQL Injection attempts*

```
/?page_id=1601 HTTP/1.0" 503 18337 "-" "Opera/9.27"
/?page_id=1601%27%20AnD%20sLeep%283%29%20ANd%20%270%27%3D%270 HTTP/1.0" 503 18337 "-" "Opera/9.27"
/?page_id=1601%26%26SlEEp%283%29 HTTP/1.0" 503 18337 "-" "Opera/9.27"
/?page_id=1601%27%20AnD%20sLeep%283%29%20ANd%20%271 HTTP/1.0" 503 18337 "-" "Opera/9.27"
/?page_id=1601%27%26%26sLEEp%283%29%26%26%271 HTTP/1.0" 503 18337 "-" "Opera/9.27"
/?page_id=1601%00%27%7C%7CSLeeP%283%29%26%26%271 HTTP/1.0" 503 18337 "-" "Opera/9.27"
/?page_id=1601%20AnD%20BeNChMaRK%282999999%2CMD5%28NoW%28%29%29%29 HTTP/1.0" 503 18337 "-" "Opera/9.27"
/?page_id=1601%26%26BeNChMaRK%282999999%2CMD5%28NoW%28%29%29%29 HTTP/1.0" 503 18337 "-" "Opera/9.27"
/?page_id=1601%27%20aND%20BeNChMaRK%282999999%2CMd5%28NoW%28%29%29%29%20AnD%20%271 HTTP/1.0" 503 18337 "-"
/?page_id=1601%27%26%26BeNChMaRK%282999999%2CmD5%28NOW%28%29%29%29%26%26%271 HTTP/1.0" 503 18337 "-" "Oper
/?page_id=1601%20or%20(1,2)=(select*from(select%20name_const(CHAR(111,108,111,108,111,115,104,101,114),1),
```

To decode, you can use websites that decode it, or use tools like Burp Suite. After dropping the URL encoded strings into Burp Suite's Decoder (Figure 14-4), you can see the use of SLEEP & BENCHMARK commands.

FIGURE 14-4 *Decoded strings reveal blind SQLi attempts*

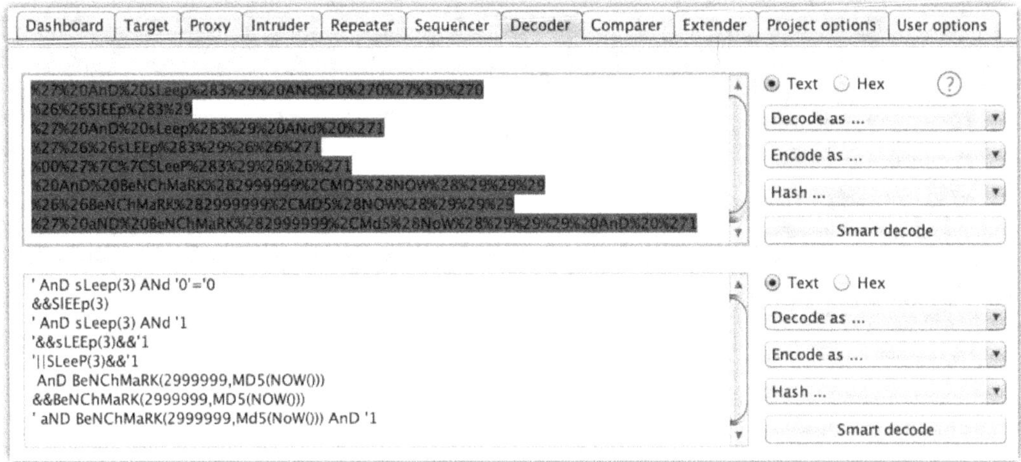

This attack is called a blind SQL Injection, since upon execution of the SQL command nothing is returned to the attacker. In order for the attacker to get an indication that the injection was successfully, he asks MySQL to do something that takes a noticeable amount of time to complete. That time is used as the feedback to the attacker. Typical commands used in time-based blind attacks are SLEEP() and BENCHMARK().

Apache's error.log File

The error.log file, located in the /var/log/apache2/ directory, will show you errors from PHP (Figure 14-5). Notice the repeated username enumeration attempts from 185.220.70.154 is generating PHP Warnings for **Invalid argument** with the query string of **author=1**.

FIGURE 14-5 *Entries in the error.log file*

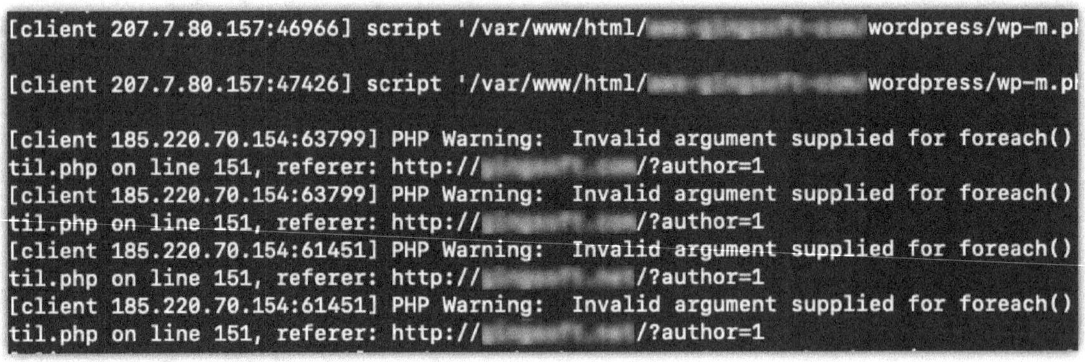

MySQL's error.log File

The error.log file, located in the /var/log/mysql/ directory, can show you failed access attempts like this one in Figure 14-6.

FIGURE 14-6 *Access denied entry in the error.log file*

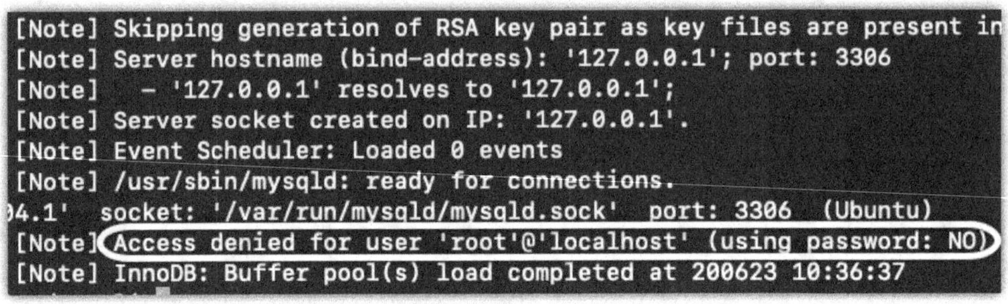

Operating System Log Files

Depending on the operating system that you've chosen, the names and locations for the logs will be slightly different. For Linux based systems, you should start in the /var/log/ directory.

Linux auth.log File

The auth.log file, located in the /var/log/ directory, will show you commands that have executed. In Figure 14-7 you can see that updates were performed, followed by a reboot.

FIGURE 14-7 *Entries in the auth.log file*

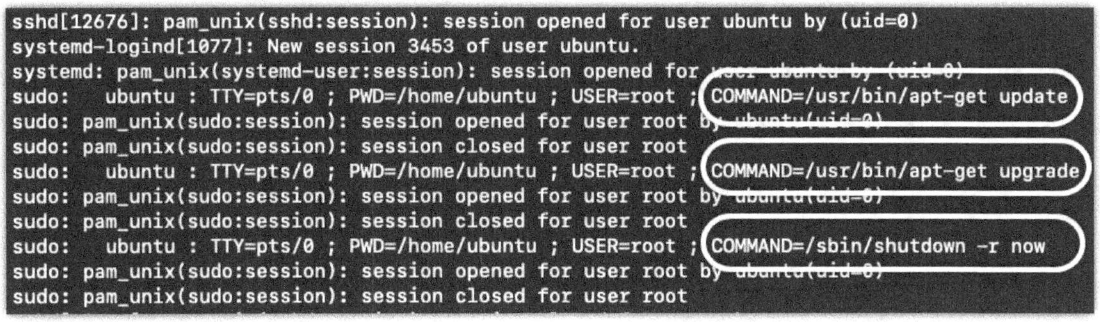

```
sshd[12676]: pam_unix(sshd:session): session opened for user ubuntu by (uid=0)
systemd-logind[1077]: New session 3453 of user ubuntu.
systemd: pam_unix(systemd-user:session): session opened for user ubuntu by (uid=0)
sudo:   ubuntu : TTY=pts/0 ; PWD=/home/ubuntu ; USER=root ; COMMAND=/usr/bin/apt-get update
sudo: pam_unix(sudo:session): session opened for user root by ubuntu(uid=0)
sudo: pam_unix(sudo:session): session closed for user root
sudo:   ubuntu : TTY=pts/0 ; PWD=/home/ubuntu ; USER=root ; COMMAND=/usr/bin/apt-get upgrade
sudo: pam_unix(sudo:session): session opened for user root by ubuntu(uid=0)
sudo: pam_unix(sudo:session): session closed for user root
sudo:   ubuntu : TTY=pts/0 ; PWD=/home/ubuntu ; USER=root ; COMMAND=/sbin/shutdown -r now
sudo: pam_unix(sudo:session): session opened for user root by ubuntu(uid=0)
sudo: pam_unix(sudo:session): session closed for user root
```

Summary

Now that you know where to look for security events, you can identify what the tactics and techniques that the attackers are using. The next step is to take action based on that information.

Chapter 15 | Stop the Attack!

Overview

You are monitoring your log files and find failed login attempts, a bunch of 404 errors, repeated xml-rpc entries. You take action by breaking the attacker's connection to the server and stopping the attack.

Null Routing

The fastest way to stop an attack from a single attacker, is to null route the attackers IP address (or entire subnet) to the loopback interface. The TCP SYN packets will reach your server, but the SYN ACK will get lost on the way back to the attacker because the loopback interface doesn't have a route back to the attacker (or anywhere else for that matter). So, the TCP 3-way handshake never completes thus stopping the attack at the network layer.

Null routing doesn't require a service to be restarted in order for this to work. It's a single command and works the second that you press the return key. To add a null route for an attacker coming from 3.15.195.17, type **route add 3.15.195.17 gw 127.0.0.1 lo** at the command prompt. To view the routing table, type **netstat -nr**.

```
root@ip-172-31-60-168:/var/log/apache2# route add 3.15.195.17 gw 127.0.0.1 lo
root@ip-172-31-60-168:/var/log/apache2# netstat -nr
Kernel IP routing table
Destination      Gateway           Genmask          Flags    MSS Window  irtt
Iface
0.0.0.0          172.31.48.1       0.0.0.0          UG         0 0        0 eth0
```

```
3.15.195.17      127.0.0.1        255.255.255.255 UGH        0 0          0 lo
172.31.48.0      0.0.0.0          255.255.240.0   U          0 0          0 eth0
```

The attacker's view of the null route. The attacker's attempts to reach to your WordPress site, now receive a **Connection timed out** message.

```
ec2-user@kali:~$ curl http://13.82.176.238
curl: (28) Failed to connect to 13.82.176.238 port 80: Connection timed out
```

Blacklisting

In order to blacklist partial or full IP addresses, subnets, user-agent strings, use either the apache2.conf or .htaccess files. Remember the **Order Deny,Allow** directive defaults to allowing access until you explicitly deny. If you make changes, remember to restart Apache for the changes to take effect.

```
<Directory /var/www/html/ >
AllowOverride None
SetEnvIfNoCase User-Agent 'Attacker User Agent 1337' evil
Order Deny,Allow
Deny from env=evil
Deny from 126.
Deny from 125.0.0.0/8
Deny from 124.0.0.0/255.0.0.0
Deny from 121.222.33.45
Deny from darkredteam.com
Deny from .kp
```

```
</Directory>
```

Whitelisting

Whitelisting is the inverse blacklisting. Blacklist defaults to Allow, while a whitelist defaults to Deny until you explicitly allow. You do this with the Order Allow,Deny directive. If you make changes, remember to restart Apache for the changes to take effect.

```
<Directory /var/www/html/ >
AllowOverride None
SetEnvIfNoCase User-Agent 'AWPSEC UA' goodguys
Order Allow,Deny
Allow from env=goodguys
Allow from 10.128.
Allow from 10.128.0.0/9
Allow from 36.0.0.0/255.0.0.0
Allow from 64.45.67.89
Allow from awpsec.com
Allow from .org
</Directory>
```

Geo-blocking

This can be handled in a few different ways. You can research what IP subnets are assigned to each country that you wish to deny and build blacklist those subnets. There are a few drawbacks with that manually. The list could get quite unwieldy pretty quick, there are lots of subnets for an entire country. The subnets change occasionally, and you won't know it until you perform your research all over again. A better solution is to choose a plugin to do this for you.

Again, choose your plugins wisely. Another option available to those of you using a Web Application Firewall (WAF) in front of your site, is to configure geo-blocking in the WAF.

Summary

Monitor your logs to identify the attackers. If an attack is ongoing, just can stop them quickly by null routing the attackers source IP address to the loopback interface. For repeat offenders, you can begin building out your blacklist. Once your blacklist gets too large and complex, you can switch to a whitelist approach.

Chapter 16 | Restore

Overview

Good news! While you were sleeping a self-propagating zero-day exploit was released onto the Internet. Before your coffee is done brewing, you read the alerts on mobile phone. Your site has been offline for nearly 6 hours. In this moment, does panic set in or are you calm because your last several test restores were fine?

Importance of Restoring

I'm not going to bore you with a bunch of fluff about how important backups are, you've already heard it. What's more important for you is getting comfortable with restoring from the backup before you really need it. Some common questions about the restore that you should be able to answer are:

- When was the last backup?
- What exactly has been backed up (MySQL, filesystem, snapshot of the VM, etc.)?
- How much time will it take to perform the restore?
- Do you restore overtop of the existing installation or nuke from high orbit and start over?
- Can you redirect visitors to a static "We're doing some maintenance" landing page, or let them see the 404 error in their browser?

Documentation

To help you recover quickly you should document steps required to bring everything up from scratch. That documentation should be printed out and put in a place where your teammates can find it. Get a red binder and write "Emergency" or something on the spine. That may sound weird to print it; however, some people panic when things aren't going well and having the answer physically in their hand does calms them down. Calm people make calculated decisions based on reasoning and clear thinking.

Stressed out people, especially those in a leadership positions are expected to have the answers and take action quickly. When they get stressed by an event such as a server outage, that stress is compounded if they don't know what to do immediately. The answers don't come quickly because their mind is clouded by thoughts of looking stupid when people are expecting them to act decisively. The barrage of stupid thoughts rolls in.

"We have to do something!"

"What do we do now?"

"There goes my bonus!"

"I'm totally fired after this!"

Do yourself a favor, skip all those non-productive thoughts and decisively walk over and pull the red binder off of the shelf.

Test Restore Process

The objective is to stand up a second copy of your site with a public IP address so you can access it. I can restore from Amazon Web Service's (AWS) in around 15 minutes. Your times will vary depending on the size of the volume and other obvious factors like the performance of the hosting platform that you're using.

1. Login to console.aws.amazon.com

2. Under Elastic Block Store, click Volumes

3. Select the most recent snapshot of volume.

4. Select it.

5. Actions-Create Image. The result is an Amazon Machine Image (AMI).

6. Select the AMI.

7. Actions-Launch.

8. Choose an Instance Type.

9. Configure Instance Details.

    a. VPC.

    b. Subnet.

    c. Auto-assign IP enabled.

10. Add Storage = default.

11. Add Tags = none.

12. Configure Security Group

    a. Select an existing security group

13. Review and Launch the AMI

14. Launch

15. Select existing Key-Pair

16. Launch Instance

17. Check public IP

18. Change the wp_options table to use new URL root instead of the old one. Otherwise, clicking anything will send you to the other server.

    a. mysql> update wp_options set option_value = "https://<public IP address>" where option_id=1;

    b. repeat with id=2;

19. 2FA still works too! Because it's still the same key.

Other Benefits

You can use a restored clone of your WordPress site for all kinds of things:

- Perform more aggressive penetration tests where the rules of engagement can be wide open.
- Test other themes, colors, fonts without messing up your current site.
- Perform some A/B testing with a different domain name or a sub-domain.
- Restore the clone to a virtual machine with different levels of performance. If you find that your site works fine on less horsepower, you can save a little money.
- Testing Patches.

Summary

Perform a test restore and document it. Next month, do it again and update the documentation. Get familiar with how to restore your actual site as well as spinning up clones for other purposes. This effort will pay off later, when you need it most.

Chapter 17 | Patching

Overview

Brush your teeth, exercise, eat right, and patch patch patch! Yes, you've heard it long before you got here. But seriously patch as often as possible. This simple mundane task could protect you more than anything else that you've read so far.

Why is it a Big Deal?!

Short answer, it's a race! You see, when a bug, defect, or vulnerability is found in an application (e.g. WordPress, MySQL, PHP, any plugin, etc.), the developer of that application comes up with the patch. When the new patch is released, the attackers quickly reverse engineer the patch to figure out what the patch is fixing. In other words, what is different between the old version and the new version. Once the attackers pinpoint what the patch is trying to protect you from, they build an exploit to take advantage of unpatched systems. If the attackers find your site before you get around to patching, they have a higher probability of the exploit being successful.

FIGURE 17-1 *Updated WordPress, Plugins, and Themes*

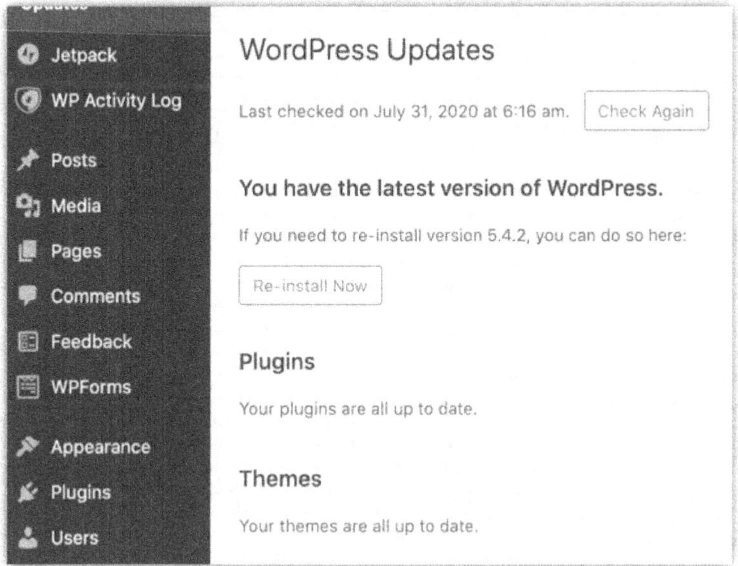

Summary

The most common excuses for not patching is either laziness, being too busy, forgetting about it, or fear of breaking your site. The fear-based excuse can be removed by restoring your site on a different server (spinning up a clone), patching the clone, and testing. You can do this in less than an hour. If all goes well, then patch your production server. Setting WordPress to Auto-update to remove the other excuses.

Chapter 18 | Web Application Firewalls (WAF)

Overview

Web Application Firewalls, or affectionally known as WAFs, provide you protection from application layer attacks such as Cross-Site Scripting (XSS), Cross-Site Request Forgery (CSRF), DDoS attack mitigation, and SQL Injection (SQLi). There are three basic types of WAF; Host-based, network-based, or cloud-based. There are several vendors that provide these services.

Host-based WAF

As the name implies, the Host-based WAF sits on the WordPress server itself. You simply install a WAF plugin and the configuration is handled though the WordPress Dashboard. The most popular one to date is Wordfence. This is the cheapest option of the three WAF types. In fact, the non-premium version is free. This is also the easiest to implement, with an implementation time of just a few minutes. The disadvantages is that you get less control than the others. If you want more control, you have to pay for the premium version, which is around $100 per year.

Network-based WAF

A network-based WAF typically runs on another server, or could be another dedicated piece of hardware that is located between your server and the Internet. The premise here is that connections from the Internet hit the WAF and then are reverse-proxied to your server or servers. The network-based WAF works fine in load balanced configurations. The drawbacks are the installation, maintenance, and cost.

Cloud-based WAF

A cloud-based WAF is the same concept as the network-based WAF from a reverse-proxy perspective. With the ever-familiar cloud utopia of not worrying about the hardware. You do typically give up a little bit on configuration options, since the WAF provider is ultimately in control of the hardware. But the speed to implement is only slightly behind that of the host-based WAF. You can literally get your WordPress site behind a WAF in under an hour. All you have to do is sign up and pay for the service ($20 per month range), point your domain's name servers to the WAF provider, install a certificate and private key on your origin server, and your off and running. Other benefits of the cloud-based WAF approach is that they usually offer Content Delivery Network (CDN), DDoS mitigation, Image optimization, caching of static content, and geo-blocking.

Summary

Each WAF type has their own pros and cons, but all of them come with an increase in protections from application layer attacks, so I encourage you to consider implementing one of them. If you're are maintaining a WordPress site for a small company with a single server and not much interaction from customers, then maybe go with the host-based plugin. If the e-commerce that your site provides is significant enough to cover a $20 per month fee, you should opt for the cloud-based WAF instead.

Appendix A | Amazon Web Services (AWS)

Why AWS?

The short answer, ultimate flexibility with very high availability! If you want control over almost every aspect of the web application, the databases, the virtual infrastructure, autoscaling, etc. You can build your own virtual servers or go directly to the new hotness, serverless! You can even connect your legacy on-prem systems into AWS to connect to your Virtual Private Cloud (VPC). Web hosting providers have come a long way, but you don't get that same level of control.

Overview of AWS Global Infrastructure

Regions

AWS is global network that is divided into Regions. Each Region is completely independent from the others. Regions are also isolated from each other. Isolation is good for security as an outbreak in one Region doesn't make the others vulnerable. The Regions are:

- Asia Pacific
    - Hong Kong (ap-east-1)
    - Mumbai (ap-south-1)
    - Seoul (ap-northeast-2)
    - Singapore (ap-southeast-1)
    - Sydney (ap-southeast-2)
    - Tokyo (ap-northeast-1)
- Canada (ca-central-1)
- Europe

- o Frankfurt (eu-central-1)
- o Ireland (eu-west-1)
- o London (eu-west-2)
- o Milan (eu-south-1)
- o Paris (eu-west-3)
- o Stockholm (eu-north-1)
- Middle East (me-south-1)
- South Africa (af-south-1)
- South America (sa-east-1)
- United States
  - o Northern Virginia (us-east-1)
  - o Ohio (us-east-2)
  - o Northern California (us-west-1)
  - o Oregon (us-west-2)

Availability Zones

Each Region has multiple Availability Zones which are connected together over low latency connections. You can think of Availability Zones as datacenters that have these characteristics:

- Physically separated inside of the Region.
- Located in areas that have a low risk of flooding.
- Power comes from multiple power grids from independent utility companies.
- Redundant connections to Tier-1 transit network providers.

The intent of all this redundancy is to maximize the uptime of resources provided by AWS. If you place your web application in multiple Availability Zones and load balance between them, you have a good chance of never going down because of a hardware failure in the AWS infrastructure.

With a solid infrastructure covered, it frees up time so you can reduce other risks such as misconfiguration, security incidents, lost credentials, data corruption.

Amazon Elastic Compute Cloud (EC2)

This is a fancy name for virtual machine. This is the virtual hardware that WordPress will be using. You can choose from:

- Type of Instance
    - General Purpose
    - Compute Optimized
    - GPU instances
    - Memory Optimized
    - Storage Optimized
- Number of CPUs
- Amount of memory
- Type and amount of storage (EBS)
- Network speed

Amazon Elastic Block Store (EBS)

Volumes

An EBS volume is the virtual hard drive where the operating system and WordPress reside. Each EBS volume is automatically replicated inside of its Availability Zone.

Snapshots

Snapshots allow for backups, restores, creating Amazon Machine Images (AMI) that can be used as a base image (aka Golden Image). If you intend on spinning up a development, running A/B testing, or quickly need a new WordPress site stood up for an event, then snapshots are how you get there quickly.

Lifecycle Manager

This feature allows you to configure a policy to schedule the creation and deletion of EBS volume snapshots on a recurring basis. That's the long way of saying automated backups.

Amazon Virtual Private Cloud (VPC)

This is your private network layer where your EC2 instances reside within AWS. You can setup your own private IPv4 address space. You also have control over:

- Subnets
- Route tables
- DHCP options
- Security groups
- Network Access Control List (aka ACL or NACL)
- Elastic IP address (public IP addresses)
- Internet Gateways (IGW)
- Network Address Translation (NAT)

Security Tools

There are many security tools and configuration options t

- **AWS WAF** – Web Application Firewall that allows you to monitor web requests that are forwarded to Amazon CloudFront distributions or an Application Load Balancer (ALB). It can can also block or allow requests based on conditions that you specify, such as the source IP addresses or patterns in the requests.

- **AWS Shield** – There are two versions of Shield (Standard and Advanced). AWS Shield Standard is automatically included at no extra cost beyond what you already pay for AWS WAF and other AWS services. AWS Shield Advanced provides expanded DDoS attack protection for Amazon EC2 instances, Elastic Load Balancing (ELB) load balancers, Amazon CloudFront distributions, and Amazon Route 53 hosted zones.

- **AWS Single Sign-On** – Control SSO access and user permissions across all your AWS accounts in AWS Organizations. It also administers access to applications that support Security Assertion Markup Language (SAML) 2.0. It offers a user portal where your users can find all their assigned AWS accounts, business applications, and custom applications in a single place.

- **Identity and Access Management (IAM)** – Centrally manage users, credentials such as access keys, and permissions that control which AWS resources users and applications can access.

- **Inspector** – Vulnerability assessment service that automatically assesses resources for vulnerabilities or deviations from best practices, and then produces a prioritized list of security findings by severity. Also includes a knowledge base of hundreds of rules mapped to common security standards and vulnerability definitions that are regularly updated by AWS security researchers.

- **Detective** – Analyze, investigate, and identify the root cause of security event or suspicious activities. Detective automatically collects log data from your AWS resources and uses machine learning, statistical analysis, and graph theory to help you visualize and conduct faster and more efficient security investigations.

- **GuardDuty** – Security monitoring service that can help to identify unexpected, unauthorized, or malicious activity in your AWS environment.

- **Secrets Manager** – Securely encrypt, store, and retrieve credentials for your databases and other services. Instead of hardcoding credentials in your apps, you can make calls to Secrets Manager to retrieve credentials whenever needed. Secrets Manager protects access to your resources and data by enabling you to rotate and manage access to your secrets.

- **Directory Service** – Set up and run Microsoft Active Directory with other AWS services such as Amazon EC2, Amazon RDS for SQL Server, Amazon FSx for Windows File Server, and AWS Single-Sign On. AWS Directory Service for Microsoft Active Directory, also known as AWS Managed Microsoft AD, enables your directory-aware workloads and AWS resources to use a managed Active Directory in the AWS Cloud

- **Artifact** – Web service that enables you to download AWS security and compliance documents such as ISO certifications and SOC reports.

- **Cognito** – User authentication and authorization for your web and mobile apps. With user pools, you can easily and securely add sign-up and sign-in functionality to your apps. With identity pools (federated identities), your apps can get temporary credentials that grant users access to specific AWS resources, whether the users are anonymous or are signed in.

Summary

There is a lot more to AWS than what I've mentioned. The point was that it has flexibility, scalability, high availability, has lots of security tools, and provides more control than that of the typical hosting providers.

Appendix B | Apache

Overview

Apache is the web server that I chose to install. Historically Apache was the majority of all web servers out there. As of late, NGINX is gaining in popularity and most newer sites are using it, but there is still a huge footprint of Apache out there. I'm saving NGINX for the next edition of this book.

Installing Apache

Before installing anything, you want to check for available updates for the Operating System. For Ubuntu you will need **sudo** for these actions, rather than typing sudo in front of every command, I prefer to use **sudo -I** once instead and skip the extra typing.

```
sudo -i
apt-get update
apt-get upgrade
shutdown -r now
```

After restarting, we now install apache2

```
apt install apache2
```

Ubuntu uses something called an Uncomplicated Firewall (aka UFW) on the host. You need to verify it's not going to be blocking the HTTP (TCP port 80) and HTTPS (TCP port 443) traffic

```
ufw app list
```

The result of that command reveals the Available Applications

```
Available applications:
  Apache
  Apache Full
  Apache Secure
  OpenSSH
```

To explore the Available applications, type **ufw app info** then the name of the application above. Start with the first one, Apache

```
ufw app info Apache
```

The result is…

```
Profile: Apache
Title: Web Server
Description: Apache v2 is the next generation of the omnipresent Apache web
server.

Port:
```
  80/tcp

Notice that port TCP 80 is open. Now take a look at **Apache Full**

```
ufw app info "Apache Full"
```

The result is…

```
Profile: Apache Full
Title: Web Server (HTTP,HTTPS)
Description: Apache v2 is the next generation of the omnipresent Apache web
server.

Ports:
  80,443/tcp
```

Notice that both TCP 80 and 443 are open in Apache Full. Now, let's see what's in Apache Secure.

```
ufw app info "Apache Secure"
```

The result is…

```
Profile: Apache Secure
Title: Web Server (HTTPS)
Description: Apache v2 is the next generation of the omnipresent Apache web
server.

Port:
  443/tcp
```

Notice that TCP 443 is open. At this point, we're good on the ports being open. Now let's verify from the Internet. We need to know the public IP address of the server. You can do this from the AWS Console or from the command line that you are currently using by typing, curl ident.me.

```
curl ident.me
```

The result will look something like this, but obviously with different IP Addresses…

```
3.12.13.37root@ip-172-16-1-1:~#
```

It contains your public IP (e.g. 3.12.13.37) followed directly by the prompt (e.g. root@ip-172-16-1-1:~#). Now if you go to http://<your IP address>, you should see the apache default page (Figure B-1).

FIGURE B-1 *Apache Default page*

Apache2 Ubuntu Default Page

It works!

This is the default welcome page used to test the correct operation of the Apache2 server after installation on Ubuntu systems. It is based on the equivalent page on Debian, from which the Ubuntu Apache packaging is derived. If you can read this page, it means that the Apache HTTP server installed at this site is working properly. You should **replace this file** (located at `/var/www/html/index.html`) before continuing to operate your HTTP server.

If you are a normal user of this web site and don't know what this page is about, this probably means that the site is currently unavailable due to maintenance. If the problem persists, please contact the site's administrator.

Configuration Overview

Ubuntu's Apache2 default configuration is different from the upstream default configuration, and split into several files optimized for interaction with Ubuntu tools. The configuration system is **fully documented in /usr/share/doc/apache2/README.Debian.gz**. Refer to this for the full documentation. Documentation for the web server itself can be found by accessing the **manual** if the `apache2-doc` package was installed on this server.

The configuration layout for an Apache2 web server installation on Ubuntu systems is as follows:

```
/etc/apache2/
|-- apache2.conf
|       `--  ports.conf
|-- mods-enabled
|       |-- *.load
|       `-- *.conf
|-- conf-enabled
|       `-- *.conf
|-- sites-enabled
|       `-- *.conf
```

- `apache2.conf` is the main configuration file. It puts the pieces together by including all remaining configuration files when starting up the web server.

- `ports.conf` is always included from the main configuration file. It is used to determine the listening ports for incoming connections, and this file can be customized anytime.

- Configuration files in the `mods-enabled/`, `conf-enabled/` and `sites-enabled/` directories contain particular configuration snippets which manage modules, global configuration fragments, or virtual host configurations, respectively.

- They are activated by symlinking available configuration files from their respective *-available/ counterparts. These should be managed by using our helpers `a2enmod`, `a2dismod`, `a2ensite`, `a2dissite`, and `a2enconf`, `a2disconf` . See their respective man pages for detailed information.

- The binary is called apache2. Due to the use of environment variables, in the default configuration, apache2 needs to be started/stopped with `/etc/init.d/apache2` or `apache2ctl`. **Calling `/usr/bin/apache2` directly will not work** with the default configuration.

If you see a similar page, then you can be confident that Apache is running. To see what version of Apache you are running, just type **apache2 -v**.

```
apache2 -v
Server version: Apache/2.4.29 (Ubuntu)
Server built:   2020-03-13T12:26:16
```

Enable Permalinks

WordPress has a feature called permalink that makes friendly looking links to pages and blog posts. This is will be needed if you get serious about Search Engine Optimization (SEO). Apache needs the **rewrite** module enabled to allow permalinks to work. To enable it you use Ubuntu's **a2enmod** script that enables the modules in apache2. When you *enable* a module in apache, you are actually creating symlinks within the **/etc/apache2/mods-enabled** directory. To disable a module, use the **a2dismod** script, which removes those symlinks. Enable the rewrite module.

```
a2enmod rewrite
```

The result of that lets you know that a restart Apache is needed for it to take effect.

```
Enabling module rewrite.
To activate the new configuration, you need to run:
  systemctl restart apache2
```

We issue the **systemctl restart apache2** command to restart the Apache service.

```
systemctl restart apache2
```

Summary

At this point, you should have a working Apache webserver up and running, albeit serving up the boring default page. The Ubuntu Uncomplicated Firewall (UFW) was opened up to allow for TCP port 80 and 443. Permalinks have been enabled to which will benefit you will any SEO. And you also learned how to enable and disable modules in Apache.

Appendix C | MySQL

Overview

The database is the heart of any meaningful web application. WordPress would be useless without it. We'll be installing MySQL using the **secure-mysql-installation** option and giving it long non-predictable password.

Installing MySQL

If you are still logged in as root, you can execute all the commands below. If you get an access denied message, type sudo in front of the commands. Or you can just type sudo -i, and not have to type sudo for every command.

```
apt install mysql-server
```

A quick word on passwords. You will be asked for a password. Make it more than 14 characters and use all of the available character sets (UPPER, lower, numb3r5, symbol$). Don't make it a dictionary word with the predictable I-wanna-be-hacker substitution cipher. You know what I mean, it's where you replace one character, like…

- a = @ or 4
- e = 3
- i = ! or 1 or |
- g = 9
- o = 0 or ()
- s = 5 or $

- $z = 2$

All modern brute force password crackers have this built in. For example, don't use a dictionary word like **August** and change a couple characters like **A** to **@**, and **s** a **5** to make **@ugu5t**. Both of these passwords weak and can be cracked easily.

Also, how many times have you tried to set a password like **@ugu5t**, but it gets denied because it wasn't long enough? To make it long enough, you just tack on some numbers to the end, like **@ugu5t2020**. This method is also used in brute force attacks, so don't do it.

When you are asked to create a password, enter something like the password below where it doesn't spell a dictionary word and isn't memorable. You will need to store this in your password manager of choice.

```
mysql password = Ha(*U&^TR^JIL2-
```

You should be presented with the option to make your installation of MySQL more secure. Definitely chose this option, it will make MySQL more secure by removing unneeded accounts

```
mysql_secure_installation
```

Answer **y** to the question

```
Securing the MySQL server deployment.

Connecting to MySQL using a blank password.
```

```
VALIDATE PASSWORD PLUGIN can be used to test passwords and improve security.
It checks the strength of password and allows the users to set only those
passwords which are secure enough. Would you like to setup VALIDATE PASSWORD
plugin?
```

```
Press y|Y for Yes, any other key for No: y
```

Answer **y** to the below question.

```
VALIDATE PASSWORD PLUGIN can be used to test passwords and improve security.
It checks the strength of password and allows the users to set only those
passwords which are secure enough. Would you like to setup VALIDATE PASSWORD
plugin?
```

```
Press y|Y for Yes, any other key for No: y
```

We will choose the **MEDIUM** option here, since we don't have a dictionary file.

```
There are three levels of password validation policy:
```

```
LOW Length >= 8
MEDIUM Length >= 8, numeric, mixed case, and special characters
STRONG Length >= 8, numeric, mixed case, special characters and dictionary
file
```

```
Please enter 0 = LOW, 1 = MEDIUM and 2 = STRONG: 1 Please set the password
for root here.
```

Set the password, by entering it twice.

```
New password:
```

```
Re-enter new password:
```

The result is…

```
Estimated strength of the password: 100
Do you wish to continue with the password provided?(Press y|Y for Yes, any
other key for No) : y
```

You want the strength of the password to be 100. If it's not, you can type **n** and retry another password. Otherwise type **y** to continue.

```
By default, a MySQL installation has an anonymous user, allowing anyone to
log into MySQL without having to have a user account created for them. This
is intended only for testing, and to make the installation go a bit smoother.
You should remove them before moving into a production environment.
```

Remove this anonymous user account, by typing y.

```
Remove anonymous users? (Press y|Y for Yes, any other key for No) : y
```

The result is…

```
Success.
```

Next you will set where you can connect and log into MySQL from. The only place that is required for this installation is **localhost**, since we are installing everything on a single server. However, more advanced installations will typically have the database separated from the web application. But until you need that, leave it at **localhost** only for security purposes by typing **y**.

```
Normally, root should only be allowed to connect from 'localhost'. This
ensures that someone cannot guess at the root password from the network.

Disallow root login remotely? (Press y|Y for Yes, any other key for No) : y
```

The result is…

```
Success.
```

Just like above, when we removed the anonymous user account, the question comes up for the test database. Remove this test database by typing **y**.

```
By default, MySQL comes with a database named 'test' that anyone can access.
This is also intended only for testing, and should be removed before moving
into a production environment.
```

```
Remove test database and access to it? (Press y|Y for Yes, any other key for
No) : y
```

The result is…

```
Dropping test database…
Success.
Removing privileges on test database… Success.
```

When asked about reloading the privilege tables, type **y**.

```
Reloading the privilege tables will ensure that all changes made so far will
take effect immediately.

Reload privilege tables now? (Press y|Y for Yes, any other key for No) : y
```

The result is…

```
Success.
```

Troubleshooting Note:

If at this point you stop, log out, restart machine, or otherwise become a regular privileged user (not sudo or root), you won't be able to log into mysql with the correct password.

```
ec2-user@ip-172-16-1-1:~$ mysql -uroot
ERROR 1698 (28000): Access denied for user 'root'@'localhost'
```

```
ec2-user@ip-172-16-1-1:~$ sudo mysql -uroot -p
Enter password:
Welcome to the MySQL monitor.  Commands end with ; or \g.


Your MySQL connection id is 8
```

Create the WordPress Database

You need to create the database that WordPress will use. I will name this one, **database4wp**. Feel free to use a different name for yours.

```
mysql> CREATE DATABASE database4wp DEFAULT CHARACTER SET utf8 COLLATE
utf8_unicode_ci;


Query OK, 1 row affected (0.00 sec)
```

With the **database4wp** database created. You need to create the MySQL user account that WordPress will use to connect to the database. In this example, the user is **stimpy42r**. You can use anything but make it at least 14 character not a dictionary word or easily guessable, I'll use **78GBVwed-6rr95**.

```
mysql> GRANT ALL ON database4wp.* TO 'stimpy42r'@'localhost' IDENTIFIED BY
'78GBVwed-6rr95';


Query OK, 0 rows affected, 1 warning (0.00 sec
```

Troubleshooting Note:

If you noticed the **0 rows affected** string in the results of the previous command. To verify that the user was actually created, we need to go to the user table in the database called mysql, not our new database named **database4wp**.

```
mysql> show databases;
+--------------------+
| Database           |
+--------------------+
| information_schema |
| database4wp        |
| mysql              |
| performance_schema |
| sys                |
+--------------------+
5 rows in set (0.00 sec)
```

```
mysql> use mysql Reading table information for completion of table and column
names You can turn off this feature to get a quicker startup with -A
```

Now that you are in the mysql database, run a select statement to show the user accounts.

```
mysql> select Host,User from user;
+-----------+------------------+
| Host      | User             |
+-----------+------------------+
| localhost | debian-sys-maint |
| localhost | stimp42r         |
```

```
| localhost | mysql.session   |
| localhost | mysql.sys       |
| localhost | root            |
+-----------+-----------------+
5 rows in set (0.00 sec)
```

Now that we've verified the user account is there. We need to flush the privileges so that mysql knows to use them.

```
mysql> flush privileges;

Query OK, 0 rows affected (0.00 sec)
```

Summary

We now have the MySQL server up and running. An empty database has been created for WordPress to use later. We created a user and set a password that WordPress will log in with. That user should only be able to login from localhost, because we used the **mysql_secure_installation** option.

Appendix D | PHP

Overview

In the previous two chapters we installed a webserver to act as the frontend, which provides content to the client. We then added a backend database to store all of the dynamic content. Now we need PHP to hook the frontend and backend together.

Installing PHP

PHP itself is pretty powerful, however you need a couple libraries to interact with MySQL and Apache. We can install PHP and the two libraries from a single command.

```
sudo apt install php libapache2-mod-php php-mysql
```

Once that completes after a few seconds, we need to tell Apache to prefer PHP files over html. Otherwise everyone who goes to your site will only see the Apache default page. We do that by editing the **dir.conf** file in the /etc/apache2/mods-enabled/ directory.

```
nano /etc/apache2/mods-enabled/dir.conf
```

It will appear similar to the code below. Notice the order from left to right of index.**html** and index.**php**. This is the order of preference. This means that if an index.html file is found, it will serve that up to the client instead of index.php.

```
<IfModule mod_dir.c>
        DirectoryIndex index.html index.cgi index.pl index.php index.xhtml
```

```
index.htm
</IfModule>
```

Move **index.php** to be the first parameter just after **DirectoryIndex**. We don't need .cgi, .pl, or .xhtml so we can delete those. We'll keep .html and .htm for now, however we don't really need them. The resulting file should look like when we are done.

```
<IfModule mod_dir.c>
        DirectoryIndex index.php index.html index.htm
</IfModule>
```

At this point Apache doesn't know that we made a change. We need to restart Apache so it will pick up the new config changes.

```
systemctl restart apache2
```

Now that Apache is looking for index.php, let's write some test php code in a file named index.php located in the /var/www/html folder.

```
/var/www/html# nano index.php
```

Write the code below into the page and save it.

```
<!DOCTYPE html>
<html>
<body>
```

```
<h1>Test PHP page</h1>

<?php
echo "the php code has executed.";
?>


</body>
</html>
```

To verify that basic PHP is operational, you can browse to the server's address and see the text "the php code has executed" in the browser. WordPress needs some additional PHP modules to provide some of its functionality. Type the command below into the console and press return.

```
apt install php-curl php-gd php-mbstring php-xml php-xmlrpc php-soap php-intl php-zip
```

Summary

PHP is now installed with the libraries needed to work with MySQL and Apache. Apache was configured to prefer index.php before index.html. You created a test page named index.php and tested from the browser.

Appendix E | WordPress

Overview

This chapter is where things start to come together. You will be installing WordPress using apt. Connect the MySQL database to WordPress, by editing the WordPress configuration file. Then you will create a golden image, so you don't have to start from scratch every time you what to spin up a new site.

Installing WordPress

The preferred way to install WordPress is with **apt** (the Advanced Package Tool). To make sure that WordPress is available in the repository, type **apt list** in the console.

```
apt list
```

The result is hundreds of entries, you can scroll back up to find it, or just look for it specifically by adding wordpress as a parameter. Type **apt list wordpress** into the console.

```
apt list wordpress
```

The result shows WordPress is available in the repository and can be installed using apt.

```
Listing... Done
wordpress/bionic 4.9.5+dfsg1-1 all
```

To install WordPress, simply type **apt-get install wordpress** in the console.

```
apt-get install wordpress
```

Type **y** or **yes** on the prompt to use some disk space for it. Then WordPress is downloaded and unpacked. You will notice a lot of things scrolling across the screen. When it completes, WordPress will be installed, however, it won't be in the directory where Apache can use it. Using the updatedb and locate commands, we can find out where it was downloaded to. Type **updatedb** into the console and press return. Once that completes, type **locate wordpress** in the console.

```
updatedb
locate wordpress
```

The result of the locate command is a huge list of every file on the Ubuntu server that contains wordpress in the filename. We are looking for where the bulk of them landed. A quick way to identify a WordPress installation is the existence of subfolders named wp-admin, wp-content, and wp-includes. If you scroll up quite a way, you should find the location of those directories under the **/usr/share** directory.

```
. . .
/usr/share/wordpress/wp-admin/index.php
. . .
/usr/share/wordpress/wp-content/plugins/index.php
. . .
/usr/share/wordpress/wp-includes/wp-db.php
. . .
```

You should also notice wordpress files in other directories such as…

```
/etc/wordpress
/etc/wordpress/htaccess
/usr/share/wordpress
/usr/share/doc/wordpress
...
/var/lib/wordpress
/var/lib/dpkg/info/wordpress-l10n.list
...
/var/lib/wordpress/wp-content
/var/lib/wordpress/wp-content/index.php /var/lib/wordpress/wp-
content/languages /var/lib/wordpress/wp-content/plugins
/var/lib/wordpress/wp-content/themes /var/lib/wordpress/wp-content/uploads
...
```

However, those aren't the droids we're looking for. We want to copy from
/usr/share/wordpress into **/var/www/html** since we know apache is configured to look into that
directory to serve up index.php. Speaking of which we want to remove the existing index.php file
we created earlier, so we are sure to use the one from WordPress.

```
cd /var/www/html
rm index.php
```

To copy WordPress **/usr/share/wordpress** into the current directory of **/var/www/html**, use the
cp command.

```
cp -a /usr/share/wordpress/. ./
```

View the directory structure type **ls -la** into the console.

```
ls -la
```

The result is…

```
drwxr-xr-x 5 root root 4096 Apr 18 13:04 .
drwxr-xr-x 3 root root 4096 Apr 17 02:48 ..
lrwxrwxrwx 1 root root 23 Apr 7 2018 .htaccess -> /etc/wordpress/htaccess
-rw-r--r-- 1 root root 10918 Apr 17 02:48 index.html
-rw-r--r-- 1 root root 418 Apr 6 2018 index.php
-rw-r--r-- 1 root root 7440 Apr 7 2018 readme.html
-rw-r--r-- 1 root root 5697 Apr 7 2018 wp-activate.php
drwxr-xr-x 9 root root 4096 Apr 18 13:04 wp-admin
-rw-r--r-- 1 root root 364 Apr 6 2018 wp-blog-header.php
-rw-r--r-- 1 root root 1627 Apr 6 2018 wp-comments-post.php
-rw-r--r-- 1 root root 2853 Apr 6 2018 wp-config-sample.php
-rw-r--r-- 1 root root 2381 Apr 7 2018 wp-config.php
drwxr-xr-x 5 root root 4096 Apr 18 13:04 wp-content
-rw-r--r-- 1 root root 3669 Apr 6 2018 wp-cron.php
drwxr-xr-x 18 root root 12288 Apr 18 13:04 wp-includes
-rw-r--r-- 1 root root 2422 Apr 6 2018 wp-links-opml.php
-rw-r--r-- 1 root root 3306 Apr 6 2018 wp-load.php
-rw-r--r-- 1 root root 36593 Apr 6 2018 wp-login.php
-rw-r--r-- 1 root root 8048 Apr 6 2018 wp-mail.php
-rw-r--r-- 1 root root 16246 Apr 6 2018 wp-settings.php
```

```
-rw-r--r-- 1 root root 30071 Apr 6 2018 wp-signup.php
-rw-r--r-- 1 root root 4620 Apr 6 2018 wp-trackback.php
-rw-r--r-- 1 root root 3065 Apr 6 2018 xmlrpc.php
```

One thing to notice from the **ls -la** command executed above is that **root** user is the owner of all the files and subdirectories. The user that Apache is running under needs access to the wordpress file structure. To locate what user that is, look at the available users in **/etc/passwd**, the user with the home directory of **/var/www** is the user that we are looking for. Type **cat /etc/passwd | grep /var/www** in the console.

```
cat /etc/passwd | grep /var/www
```

The result is…

```
www-data:x:33:33:www-data:/var/www:/usr/sbin/nologin
```

The **www-data** user is the one you want. Make the **www-data** user and group the owner of the html directory structure. Type **chown -R www-data:www-data /var/www/html** into the console.

```
chown -R www-data:www-data /var/www/html
```

Let's take a look again with **ls -la**…

```
ls -la
```

The result is…

```
drwxr-xr-x 5 www-data www-data 4096 Apr 18 13:04 .
drwxr-xr-x 3 root root 4096 Apr 17 02:48 ..
lrwxrwxrwx 1 www-data www-data 23 Apr 7 2018 .htaccess ->
/etc/wordpress/htaccess
-rw-r--r-- 1 www-data www-data 10918 Apr 17 02:48 index.html
-rw-r--r-- 1 www-data www-data 418 Apr 6 2018 index.php
-rw-r--r-- 1 www-data www-data 7440 Apr 7 2018 readme.html
-rw-r--r-- 1 www-data www-data 5697 Apr 7 2018 wp-activate.php
drwxr-xr-x 9 www-data www-data 4096 Apr 18 13:04 wp-admin
-rw-r--r-- 1 www-data www-data 364 Apr 6 2018 wp-blog-header.php
-rw-r--r-- 1 www-data www-data 1627 Apr 6 2018 wp-comments-post.php
-rw-r--r-- 1 www-data www-data 2853 Apr 6 2018 wp-config-sample.php
-rw-r--r-- 1 www-data www-data 2381 Apr 7 2018 wp-config.php
drwxr-xr-x 5 www-data www-data 4096 Apr 18 13:04 wp-content
-rw-r--r-- 1 www-data www-data 3669 Apr 6 2018 wp-cron.php
drwxr-xr-x 18 www-data www-data 12288 Apr 18 13:04 wp-includes
-rw-r--r-- 1 www-data www-data 2422 Apr 6 2018 wp-links-opml.php
-rw-r--r-- 1 www-data www-data 3306 Apr 6 2018 wp-load.php
-rw-r--r-- 1 www-data www-data 36593 Apr 6 2018 wp-login.php
-rw-r--r-- 1 www-data www-data 8048 Apr 6 2018 wp-mail.php
-rw-r--r-- 1 www-data www-data 16246 Apr 6 2018 wp-settings.php
-rw-r--r-- 1 www-data www-data 30071 Apr 6 2018 wp-signup.php
-rw-r--r-- 1 www-data www-data 4620 Apr 6 2018 wp-trackback.php
-rw-r--r-- 1 www-data www-data 3065 Apr 6 2018 xmlrpc.php
```

At this point WordPress is installed in a directory where Apache can serve it up and the user account that Apache is running under, www-data, has the appropriate rights.

WordPress Configuration File

Now it's time to configure WordPress to use the MySQL database. The file used for that is **wp-config.php** in the **/var/www/html** directory.

Which wp-config.php file to use

The existing wp-config.php isn't the one you want to use. This version of the config file is for servers that contain more than one website, which we don't want for a number of reasons. You can tell because there is no place in this file to define the SECURE_AUTH_KEY and SECURE_AUTH_SALT values. Type **cat wp-config.php**.

```
cat wp-config.php
```
The result is…

```
<?php
/***
 * WordPress's Debianised default master config file
 * Please do NOT edit and learn how the configuration works in
 * /usr/share/doc/wordpress/README.Debian
 ***/

/* Look up a host-specific config file in
 * /etc/wordpress/config-<host>.php or /etc/wordpress/config-<domain>.php
 */
```

```php
$debian_server = preg_replace('/:.*/', "", $_SERVER['HTTP_HOST']);
$debian_server = preg_replace("/[^a-zA-Z0-9.\-]/", "", $debian_server);
$debian_file = '/etc/wordpress/config-'.strtolower($debian_server).'.php';
/* Main site in case of multisite with subdomains */
$debian_main_server = preg_replace("/^[^.]*\./", "", $debian_server);
$debian_main_file = '/etc/wordpress/config-
'.strtolower($debian_main_server).'.php';

if (file_exists($debian_file)) {
    require_once($debian_file);
    define('DEBIAN_FILE', $debian_file);
} elseif (file_exists($debian_main_file)) {
    require_once($debian_main_file);
    define('DEBIAN_FILE', $debian_main_file);
} elseif (file_exists("/etc/wordpress/config-default.php")) {
    require_once("/etc/wordpress/config-default.php");
    define('DEBIAN_FILE', "/etc/wordpress/config-default.php");
} else {
    header("HTTP/1.0 404 Not Found");
    echo "Neither <b>$debian_file</b> nor <b>$debian_main_file</b> could be
found. <br/> Ensure one of them exists, is readable by the webserver and
contains the right password/username.";
    exit(1);
}


/* Default value for some constants if they have not yet been set
   by the host-specific config files */
if (!defined('ABSPATH'))
```

```php
    define('ABSPATH', '/usr/share/wordpress/');
if (!defined('WP_CORE_UPDATE'))
    define('WP_CORE_UPDATE', false);
if (!defined('WP_ALLOW_MULTISITE'))
    define('WP_ALLOW_MULTISITE', true);
if (!defined('DB_NAME'))
    define('DB_NAME', 'wordpress');
if (!defined('DB_USER'))
    define('DB_USER', 'wordpress');
if (!defined('DB_HOST'))
    define('DB_HOST', 'localhost');
if (!defined('WP_CONTENT_DIR') && !defined('DONT_SET_WP_CONTENT_DIR'))
    define('WP_CONTENT_DIR', '/var/lib/wordpress/wp-content');

/* Default value for the table_prefix variable so that it doesn't need to
   be put in every host-specific config file */
if (!isset($table_prefix)) {
    $table_prefix = 'wp_';
}


if (isset($_SERVER['HTTP_X_FORWARDED_PROTO']) &&
$_SERVER['HTTP_X_FORWARDED_PROTO'] == 'https')
    $_SERVER['HTTPS'] = 'on';


require_once(ABSPATH . 'wp-settings.php');
?>
```

Again, you are only interested in a single website per server to minimize risk and provide maximum flexibility, so we don't want this version of the configuration file. Rename this config file to something else like **wp-config-multi.php**. Then copy the **wp-config-sample.php** as **wp-config.php** as it is more suited for running a single site on a server.

```
mv wp-config.php wp-config-multi.php
cp wp-config-sample.php wp-config.php
```

Now looking at this version of the configuration file by typing **cat wp-config.php**, you should notice there are configuration settings for the database (marked in **bold**) as well as unique keys and salts for authentication.

```
cat wp-config.php
```

The result is…

```
<?php
/**
 * The base configuration for WordPress
 *
 * The wp-config.php creation script uses this file during the
 * installation. You don't have to use the web site, you can
 * copy this file to "wp-config.php" and fill in the values.
 *
 * This file contains the following configurations:
 *
 * * MySQL settings
```

```php
 * * Secret keys
 * * Database table prefix
 * * ABSPATH
 *
 * @link https://codex.wordpress.org/Editing_wp-config.php
 *
 * @package WordPress
 */


// ** MySQL settings - You can get this info from your web host ** //
/** The name of the database for WordPress */
define('DB_NAME', 'database_name_here');


/** MySQL database username */
define('DB_USER', 'username_here');


/** MySQL database password */
define('DB_PASSWORD', 'password_here');


/** MySQL hostname */
define('DB_HOST', 'localhost');


/** Database Charset to use in creating database tables. */
define('DB_CHARSET', 'utf8');


/** The Database Collate type. Don't change this if in doubt. */
define('DB_COLLATE', '');
```

```php
/**#@+
 * Authentication Unique Keys and Salts.
 *
 * Change these to different unique phrases!
 * You can generate these using the {@link https://api.wordpress.org/secret-key/1.1/salt/ WordPress.org secret-key service}
 * You can change these at any point in time to invalidate all existing
cookies. This will force all users to have to log in again.
 *
 * @since 2.6.0
 */
define('AUTH_KEY', 'put your unique phrase here');
define('SECURE_AUTH_KEY', 'put your unique phrase here');
define('LOGGED_IN_KEY', 'put your unique phrase here');
define('NONCE_KEY', 'put your unique phrase here');
define('AUTH_SALT', 'put your unique phrase here');
define('SECURE_AUTH_SALT', 'put your unique phrase here');
define('LOGGED_IN_SALT', 'put your unique phrase here');
define('NONCE_SALT', 'put your unique phrase here');

/**#@-*/

/**
 * WordPress Database Table prefix.
 *
 * You can have multiple installations in one database if you give each
 * a unique prefix. Only numbers, letters, and underscores please!
 */
```

```
$table_prefix = 'wp_';

/**
 * For developers: WordPress debugging mode.
 *
 * Change this to true to enable the display of notices during development.
 * It is strongly recommended that plugin and theme developers use WP_DEBUG *
in their development environments.
 *
 * For information on other constants that can be used for debugging,
 * visit the Codex.
 *
 * @link https://codex.wordpress.org/Debugging_in_WordPress
 */
define('WP_DEBUG', false);

/* That's all, stop editing! Happy blogging. */

/** Absolute path to the WordPress directory. */
if ( !defined('ABSPATH') )
      define('ABSPATH', dirname(__FILE__) . '/');

/** Sets up WordPress vars and included files. */
require_once(ABSPATH . 'wp-settings.php');
```

Generate the unique keys

The first thing you need to do is generate unique keys and salt values.

```
curl -s https://api.wordpress.org/secret-key/1.1/salt/
```

The result are four key and salt value pairs.

- AUTH_KEY and AUTH_SALT
- SECURE_AUTH_KEY and SECURE_AUTH_SALT
- LOGGED_IN_KEY and LOGGED_IN_SALT
- NONCE_KEY and NONCE_SALT

```
define('AUTH_KEY',
'5:IU$hf(MwDhEgAlA6Z]c$x`wrsbD=;|)B%[+Q?`oKX%!5FKqENGyLh}p3{`s`CX');
define('SECURE_AUTH_KEY',  'd/)7*/x|Lv2_+GtGDe,o+D57Q+vWB5PacI=5G](QsZ2X-
1+ksnYW-Z>H]_qR}{-<');
define('LOGGED_IN_KEY',  'meA{$RoG!%s*XC Z!39Jm!7QF`d8Fp)y)|Y9*)
|PT+L(F@GItFdBL^4#0h3)K&q');
define('NONCE_KEY',
'UbYv>k%2d%`^$b{G,u/^?LK&zza`J(xrn|%~`AO~#r{Zk*M+u&C+Qo.<-} q+t00');
define('AUTH_SALT',  'A+D,Y7E+Qi6m'/Uae9@EO~nA#m-#-pzPu5;i/HAm!n#W)TGe=L
^i/e38O])_KF%0');
define('SECURE_AUTH_SALT',  'XT)NoBz4[|JiM/@-ulu-zI/fxh&I@aS+^J:YC!Tk+JaB-
hb0nJf K4VN2TFCzTz.');
define('LOGGED_IN_SALT',
'9ADnHuIm[GFe0oUOPy:DZo$/%m}+7|mSYOI,wZkiwXbxMv`(2xXBLMKpU`Lz+Q^Y');
define('NONCE_SALT',
'UwP@PT8QY:;/Qlt/b+t|YO_XJ;3(m#uTHiYbJc!P48=RE$lQ^p.7r>2Nmbjv;q9m');
```

Copy those lines from AUTH_KEY thru NONCE_SALT before opening the wp-config.php. Because you will be pasting those lines in place of the existing lines that look like this…

```
define('AUTH_KEY', 'put your unique phrase here');
define('SECURE_AUTH_KEY', 'put your unique phrase here');
define('LOGGED_IN_KEY', 'put your unique phrase here');
define('NONCE_KEY', 'put your unique phrase here');
define('AUTH_SALT', 'put your unique phrase here');
define('SECURE_AUTH_SALT', 'put your unique phrase here');
define('LOGGED_IN_SALT', 'put your unique phrase here');
define('NONCE_SALT', 'put your unique phrase here');
```

Use nano or your editor of choice to open up wp-config.php for editing.

```
nano wp-config.php
```

To remove the existing lines in **nano** press **Ctrl+K** with the cursor on the line that you want to remove. Which is way easier than pressing the delete key a few hundred times. When all of the example lines are deleted, paste in your unique values.

Connection to MySQL

Remember, earlier I used these values when setting up the database for WordPress in the MySQL chapter?

- Database = **database4wp**
- Username = **stimpy42r**

- Password = **78GBVwed-6rr95**

- Hostname = **localhost**

Those values get used in the wp-config.php file. The value for the database (database4wp) goes into the DB_NAME variable. The username value (stimpy42r) goes into DB_USER variable. The password (78GBVwed-6rr95) goes into the DB_PASSWORD variable. And the DB_HOST should be localhost.

```
// ** MySQL settings - You can get this info from your web host ** //
/** The name of the database for WordPress */
define('DB_NAME', 'database4wp');


/** MySQL database username */
define('DB_USER', 'stimpy42r');


/** MySQL database password */
define('DB_PASSWORD', '78GBVwed-6rr95');


/** MySQL hostname */
define('DB_HOST', 'localhost');
```


WordPress Administrator Account

Now at this point you can head back to the browser and finish the setup by browsing to the IP address of the server (Figure E-1). You will be creating the Site Title (not the domain name), The admin username, and strong password.

Remember! DO NOT USE **admin**, **wpadmin**, **wp-admin** or anything else for a username that is easy to guess by googling you or your company name!

FIGURE E-1 *WordPress Setup*

Welcome

Welcome to the famous five-minute WordPress installation process! Just fill in the information below and you'll be on your way to using the most extendable and powerful personal publishing platform in the world.

Information needed

Please provide the following information. Don't worry, you can always change these settings later.

Site Title	Gingsoft WP Example
Username	Spaceghost
	Usernames can have only alphanumeric characters, spaces, underscores, hyphens, periods, and the @ symbol.
Password	8h7y6ging$D%%^k0Oo — Hide
	Strong
	Important: You will need this password to log in. Please store it in a secure location.
Your Email	someone@gingsoft.com
	Double-check your email address before continuing.
Search Engine Visibility	Discourage search engines from indexing this site
	It is up to search engines to honor this request.

Install WordPress

Golden Image

At this point, this site is as clean as it's ever going to be. You will want to create a snapshot of the volume in AWS. So, if something goes horrible wrong with your site you can fall back to here and not have to start from scratch. Also, this provides a jump start the next time you need some other site spun up. Obviously, usernames, keys, and salts will need to be changed, but that's easy stuff and much faster than going through the entire install process again.

Summary

You now have a functioning WordPress site. It has an administrator user account that isn't easily guessable. And you now have a golden image to use as a fallback for this site and a jump start for your next site.

Appendix F | Certbot

Overview

Up to this point your WordPress site in only setup for HTTP, which isn't secure and is frowned upon by most modern browsers. The UFW is configured to allow TCP port 443, so all you need now is a TLS certificate for your domain name.

If you're wondering why we took the golden image already and didn't wait until this chapter was over with, it's because every new site will have its own unique certificate (public and private keys) for the domain name. Theoretically, you could make another golden image after this over, but it will only be good for this domain name as a brand-new site. You should be making snapshots of your site later, which contains your site's content, themes, plugins, and modifications you've made. Restoring from point will make much more sense.

certbot.eff.org

If you already have an existing certificate for your site from another certificate authority (CA), then you can skip this chapter. I prefer certbot.eff.org which is free and updates automatically and is super easy get going quickly. Open up your browser and head over to **https://certbot.eff.org**.

FIGURE F-1 *The Certbot.eff.org site*

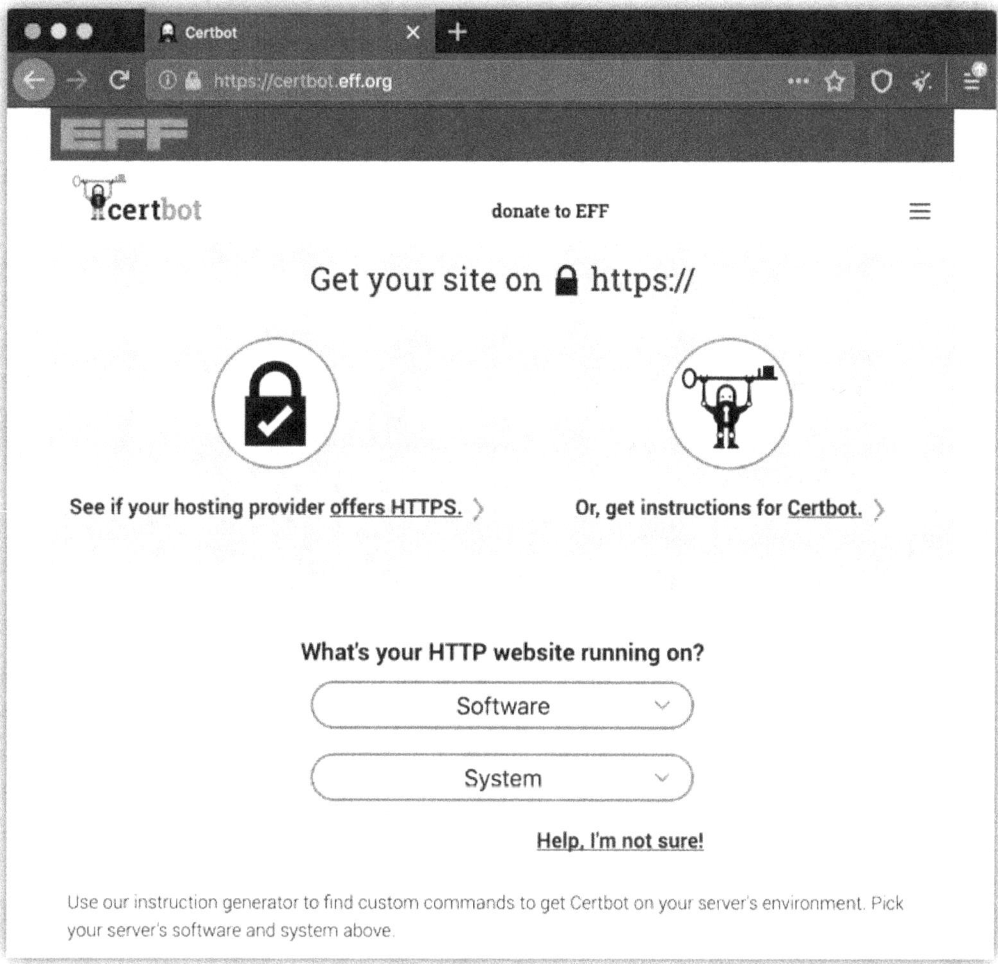

I've installed Apache on Ubuntu version 18.04 LTS, you might be using a different version. Click the **Software** button and select **Apache**. Then click the **System** button and select the version that you installed. Then scroll down to reveal the instructions you need to install Certbot on your server. Follow the instructions on the site.

FIGURE F-2 *Steps 1 and 2*

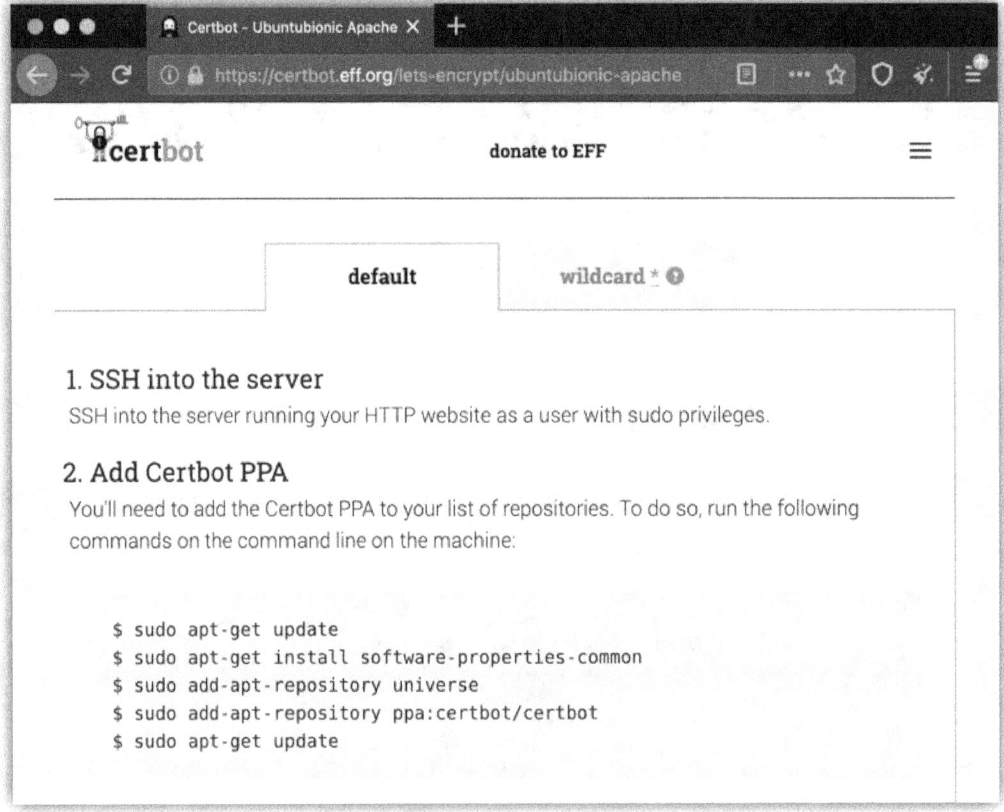

FIGURE F-3 *Steps 3 and 4*

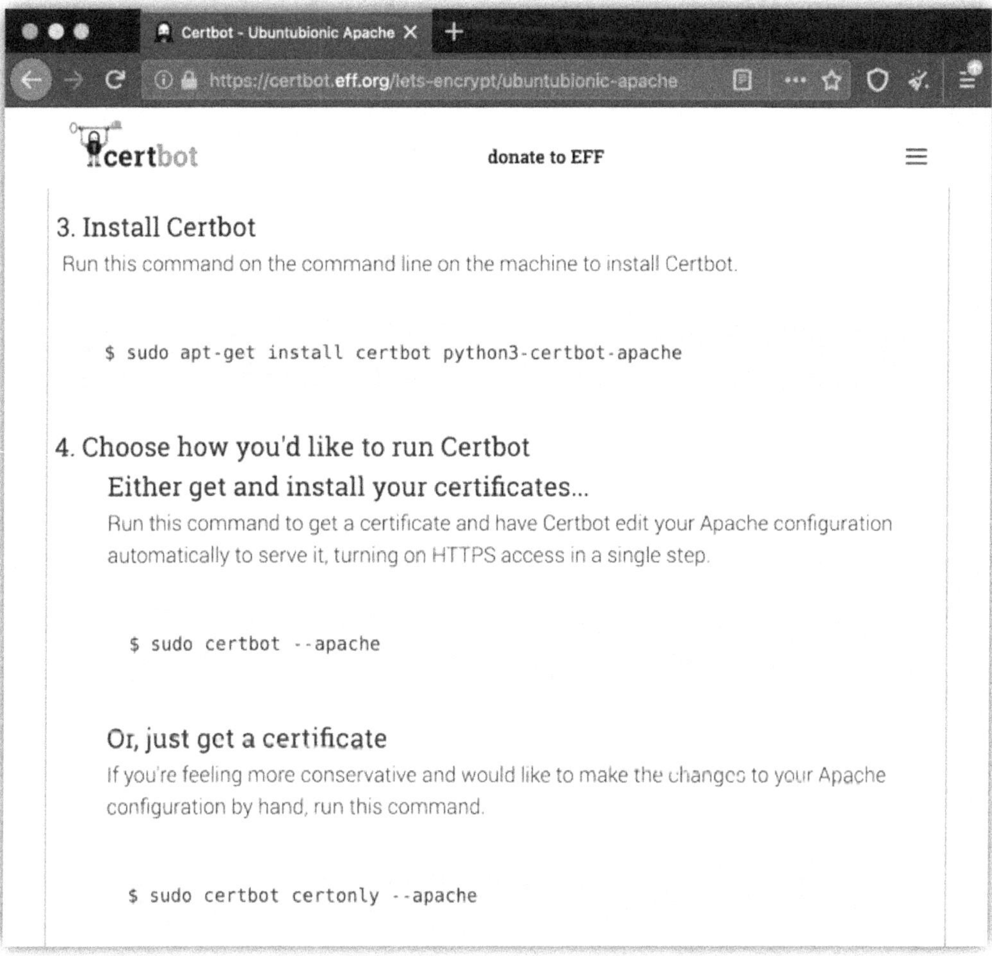

FIGURE F-4 *Steps 5 and 6*

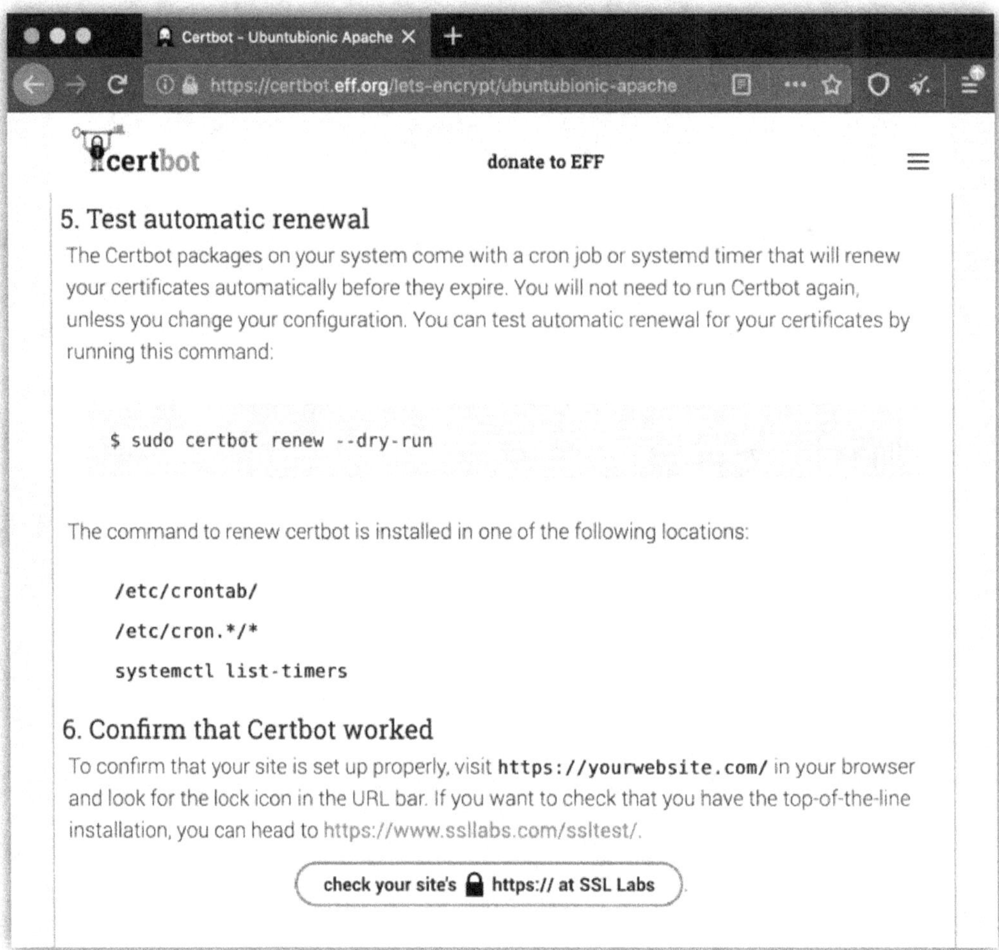

Summary

Your site is now functioning over HTTPS which secures communication between the browser and the server.

Index

www.ingramcontent.com/pod-product-compliance
Lightning Source LLC
Chambersburg PA
CBHW080903160726
48000CB00009B/2839